A MAN LEARNS

A MAN LEARNS

Mostly True Memories and Musings

✦ ✦ ✦

Donald M. Hall

SYREN BOOK COMPANY
Minneapolis

Most Syren books are available at special quantity discounts
for bulk purchases for sales promotions, premiums, fund-raising,
and educational needs. For details, write

Syren Book Company
Special Sales Department
5120 Cedar Lake Road
Minneapolis, Minnesota 55416

Published by
Syren Book Company LLC
5120 Cedar Lake Road
Minneapolis, Minnesota 55416

Printed in the United States of America on acid-free paper

ISBN-13: 978-0-929636-42-9
ISBN-10: 0-929636-42-2

LCCN 2005924966

Cover design by Kyle G. Hunter
Book design by Wendy Holdman

To order additional copies of this book see the form
at the back of this book or go to www.itascabooks.com

For Margaret, Rachel,
Peter, and Marcellus

Who used to ask me to tell them stories
and I couldn't think of any.

Contents

A MAN LEARNS

Origins

MOTHER WAS BORN with the caul tight around her face. There was some question whether she would live, her father told her later, but he pulled the membrane free, massaged her ribs, and she coughed her first breath. "Learned how to do it with the calves," he said. Their farm was just outside the little hamlet of Forada in west-central Minnesota, six miles from the town of Alexandria. It was the middle of February, 1903. Snow falls deep at that time of the year, so the ride to town must have been difficult.

Like so many of that era, my grandparents' house was a two-story frame structure with a front porch across the long side facing the evening sun. Downhill and a little to the east stood a barn big enough to hold a team of horses, about eight cows, and a bull. Beyond lay serene Maple Lake surrounded by pasture and woods. The patriarch of this pleasant acreage, a heavy-boned man with a brush mustache, had some modest note among the farmers in the area since he was the first to build a wooden stave silo. He kept pigs and chickens and used horses for fieldwork. Once, a cow sank slowly in the quicksand slough in the pasture. "No time to get the horse. No way to reach a rope to the cow," he said. "There was nothing I could do but watch it disappear. It bawled to the heavens." Then he added, "That was a tough day. Couldn't afford to lose a cow like that." When work was done he relaxed in his rocker and read the socialist newspaper, *An Appeal to Reason*.

"Put that away," Grandmother admonished whenever she saw the paper. "What if somebody saw you reading that?" But he read it anyway. He had a curious, independent mind. His wife, a former school teacher, knew formal learning but didn't share his willingness to explore alternative ideas. She kept a fussy-clean house, grew vegetables in the garden outside, and in back, near the outhouse, harvested the fruit of a half dozen apple trees. They loved their farm. Bought it with their own money but only after he had first visited North Dakota in search of cheaper land. "No trees out there," he said at the time. "Not enough to build a house," and he returned and chose instead this verdant setting in Minnesota lake country. He was forty years old, his new bride twenty-five.

There were three children in the family, all girls. Lucy was three years older than mother and Lola, nine years younger. Mother's first name was Lura, which made the trio sound like a melodic lullaby, but she was called by her second name, Icyleen. Her parents had picked it out of a newspaper someplace and liked the sound of it. About a half mile from the house stood a one-room school Mother spoke of often. She liked it because she got to learn lessons in advance by listening to students in the higher grades recite answers. When she was idle, the teacher had her help others with their work.

Mother loved that farm as much as her parents did. She didn't say it, but I know it from the story of her dream told many years later after Grandfather died. In the sleepy mists,

Grandma and Grandpa Morris, Mother, Aunt Lucy. Forada, Minnesota, ca. 1906.

he was sitting on the branch of a tree overhanging Maple Lake, and he invited her to come and join him. She was on the shore, unsure of his invitation; it didn't look quite safe. "Come," he said, "come and join me. Everything's OK." And then she felt calm and reassured and moved toward him almost as though she were joining him in heaven. "It was a lovely dream," she said without further interpretation. "He seemed so content."

When Mother was eleven, the family moved to nearby Alexandria. They had to, she said, because Grandfather had been injured in a runaway. "He was driving the wagon and something strange spooked the horses. They bolted, and he was thrown from the wagon." From the ground he looked up and saw a car drive off. He recovered physically, but his confidence was shaken. He couldn't get up in the wagon and drive again. Had it happened many years later a lawyer would have advised bringing suit, of course, but there was no such idea in that earlier America. So the family bought a house in town with extra bedrooms and took in roomers. Grandfather did odd carpentry jobs.

Mother said she was French when asked, and sometimes when not asked. She insisted on being French. Her father was French, that was pretty certain. He came from a community of French Canadians that had settled near Wells, Minnesota, close to the Iowa border. His last name was Morris, but it was supposed to be Maurice, Mother said, and it had been anglicized by a Canadian official when Grandfather's ancestors immigrated. They must have felt their identity was secure, those ancestors, and that a name change couldn't deny who they were. Or was it that freedom in the new world was more important than an accurate name? Anyway, they accepted the name and kept their French language and cultural habits intact. Grandfather's mother came from a family named Jerome, a French Canadian name that goes back in family history to the 1700s.

Grandmother, on my mother's side, had the last name of Flesch, a decidedly German-sounding name, and her mother's maiden name was Esch, which the record shows came from Cologne, Germany. The Flesches were from the town of Morbach in Alsace-Lorraine, and Mother said it depended on who won the most recent war whether it was part of France or Germany. Grandmother was born of those descendants in Volny, Iowa, a tiny village in the northeastern part of the state.

My people are French, Mother said, ignoring these possible German connections, but since she was fully French on one side and probably half French on the other, it's understandable that she might want to simplify. She had black hair and skin that tanned, like her French father's, and she was his pet. Perhaps that influenced the facts.

Grandmother and Grandfather were both from families of twelve children, so Mother had uncounted cousins, none of whom we now know anything about. The numbers explain birth control at the time.

My French grandfather was Catholic by birth, but as an adult wasn't much interested in going to church. How he got to this cavalier attitude, we don't know, but at the time of his death he was buried in the Catholic Church. Grandmother's family, the immigrants from Cologne and Alsace-Lorraine, had been Catholic also, but when the Flesches settled in tiny Volny, they found it difficult to attend mass regularly as the closest church was miles away. One spring, perhaps because the slush and mud were too deep—or maybe for some other reason, we don't know—they failed to get to church for confession and communion during the Lenten season (their "Easter duty"). A few weeks later they arrived at church, bringing with them their daughter who had just died, and asked for a Catholic requiem burial. The priest reminded them of their Lenten transgression and refused. Mortified, they never attended a Catholic church again. Grandmother, in time, joined the Congregational Church.

So, Mother, a product of a nominally Catholic father and a Congregationalist mother, attended the Congregational church when she moved to Alexandria. She learned never to

smoke and to be suspicious of alcohol. She loved dancing and
playing cards, so those must have been acceptable, and later,
after she married, she learned to like a little brandy almost
every night, although she never would admit it. It helped clear
her throat, she said.

While attending high school in Alexandria, Mother made
friends, some of which lasted a lifetime. One summer she and
a few other girls walked about two hundred miles to the Canadian border just for fun. They got an occasional ride from
a farmer driving a hay wagon and stayed in hotels or rooming
houses along the way. Nothing bad happened. When graduation came, a dozen of her classmates agreed to keep in contact
by setting up a "chain" letter. Each would put her own writing
in the envelope and pass it on; the final recipient would get
news from the eleven others. They kept this up for more than
sixty years, almost an American record; but the columnist
Ann Landers cited a group that had gone on longer.

After high school Mother went to St. Cloud to learn to be a
teacher at St. Cloud Normal (State College). There she met
Marcellus Hall, my father, at a college dance. He sidled up
next to her on a long bench, spied a pin on the floor, picked it
up, and said, "Don't say I didn't give you anything." Not much
of an opening line, I'd say, but she recounted it fondly in later
years. He also told her his name was "Dick," and she thought
it was so for a number of months. We never did learn why
he made up a name. Perhaps he thought Marcellus sounded
too old-fashioned to a stylish college girl. Perhaps he was just
spunky from a shot of whiskey earlier that evening. If we had
asked him, I think he would have said, "I don't know. It just

happened." However, they both must have thought the little ruse endearing since they later named their firstborn Richard.

Marcellus was the fifth of ten children in a very Catholic, full-blooded German family. His name, he told us, came from a saint, as did the unusual names of his sisters, Clothilda and Evarista. These were not the encumbrances they seemed, as the three were commonly called Marce, Clo, and Evie. Grandfather, Mathew Hall, had been born in Baden, Germany. His mother died in 1878 at the age of forty-three, and four years later his father brought him and the other two children to America, direct to St. Cloud, Minnesota, where a relative had previously settled. Mathew was nineteen when he immigrated.

At the age of twenty-nine, Mathew married Anna Volz from St. Cloud. Both of her parents had come from Germany. Anna was one of nine children, the descendants of whom we now have virtually no information; such is the diffusion of forebears. She was two months short of twenty-three when she got married. It was Anna who stamped the Catholic faith firmly on her own family of ten children, although she had the support of a husband who shared her religious devotion and an equally supportive culture of Catholic attitudes in central Minnesota.

Like his three older brothers, my father, Marcellus, was working in Grandfather's retail lumberyard at the time he met my mother. They dated for seven years. She said he told her his older brothers had to get married before he could, but fortunately that reason got overruled eventually, as one of the brothers didn't get married until the age of sixty. There was also the issue of religion, she being Protestant and he Catholic.

Was there anything else? We don't know. Seven years was a long courtship.

Once she finished college Mother began teaching, one year in Austin, one year in Princeton, one in Foley, and then, tired of waiting for Dad to commit, she went off to Idaho to teach for two years. When she came back, they got serious and she taught a final year in north Minneapolis. That's a lot of moving. I wonder if she might not have been invited back to teach at some of those places. She had a controlling personality and could easily lose her temper when things weren't right. Or perhaps the headaches and insomnia that troubled her later in life were showing early symptoms. If that was the case, it's doubtful she got much helpful treatment at the time. She was smart enough, but I wonder if she was a successful teacher. When, at the age of twenty-six, I wanted to leave my job in search of more opportunity, Mother advised, "You have a good job, keep it."

Mother converted to the Catholic faith, and in 1929, at the age of twenty-six, she and Dad got married. He was two months short of his twenty-eighth birthday. Once committed, they stayed married for the rest of their lives.

St. Cloud was a town of about twenty thousand then, which means it was small enough to traverse by foot or bicycle. It was famous for its nearby granite quarries and the many businesses that cut and polished the granite. It also was the county seat for Stearns County, then known as the second most concentrated population of Catholics of anyplace in the country. It was mostly German, but there were pockets of Polish and some Irish sprinkled about. As I heard it, only Brooklyn had a higher percentage of Catholics. There were Protestants on the south side of St. Cloud, but there were almost none in the numerous small communities and dairy farms out west of town comprising the rest of the county. St. Mary's Church in downtown St. Cloud served as the cathedral of the local diocese.

The Mississippi river separated the east part of town from downtown as it rolled through a shallow gorge and under the city's main bridge. The view from that bridge caused residents to marvel when huge chunks if ice clogged the river in the spring and crashed against each other in a rush downstream, and marvel again at the tranquil beauty in the fall when the trees on either bank showed their autumn hues. There was no commerce on this part of the river, although a few miles upstream, logs were floated to a paper mill, and downstream a dam and power plant generated electricity for the area.

To the casual eye, the surrounding countryside looked the same in any direction: one farm after another, each bearing a square white house, a red barn with an arching gambrel roof, and various granaries and sheds, all painted red. Between the farmsteads lay gently rolling fields of oats, hay, and corn and, in the timbered or marshy areas, pastures with a dozen black-and-white cows grazing and sometimes drinking from a trickling creek. In this county Holsteins ranked second in population to Catholics. To the attentive eye, each farm was unique and beautiful in a simple way and compatible with its setting. Every seven miles or so, a tall steeple rose above the trees, indicating a Catholic church, a nearby bar, a post office, and a community of houses. These farms and towns needed lumber to improve and fix what they had, and to grow. Grandfather's lumber business would supply them, and Marce enjoyed the work. He and Icyleen moved into a new, two-story, three-bedroom house and settled in St. Cloud, on the north side, eight blocks from downtown.

They had five children:

> Richard, born August 3, 1930
> Yvonne, born May 11, 1934
> Donald, born September 1, 1937
> Robert, born January 4, 1939
> Jerome, born January 13, 1944

I was the middle one, overlooked, of course.

Don, Marcellus (holding Jerome), Richard, Icyleen, Yvonne, and Bob Hall, ca. 1944.

Of Life

MY CRIB WAS CONFINING, I know that, but it had slats that let in light and sound, and it was open on top. On spring mornings the window would be up, and I could hear sparrows fluttering and flitting in the vines covering the screen, chirping an excited conversation. Bits of sunshine popped through the leaves and sparkled the room. And I remember—yes, I remember clearly—that the noise and light were carried into my room by a cool warming breeze that only spring delivers. That would place it before my second birthday, or my third, I can't be sure, but the conditions pleased my senses, I know that, and I was happy. When I stood and held the top rail, I could see the landscape of my room: green rugs, distant pictures. The crib did not contain me; it only kept me from falling.

There was fun, too. Once my younger brother, in a crib across the room, sprayed the air while Mother was changing his diaper. That unexpected geyser made Mother laugh, and then we laughed with her, ribald childish giggles that we kept going because the sound of laughter itself was so much fun.

I remember my sleeper, a little bunting sack that zipped up tight to my neck. No sleeves. My arms were confined, as was everything except my head. It will keep him comfortable, Mother surely thought, and snug. She zipped me up and gave me a reassuring, upbeat "good night" as she left the room. I did not like that sack; I could not move my arms.

I was on my stomach with my head to one side, hands down along my body. I could sleep all right, but it didn't seem comfortable. In the middle of the night I wanted to change my head to the other side. With no hands to help I had to lift from the neck. Impulsively, I thought I should try and see if I could do it. Halfway across, my undeveloped strength gave out and my head dropped and came to rest on my nose. The air passage was squeezed. I could hardly inhale. Fear of death grabs even so small a mind. I felt I might die. Then, again on impulse, I raised myself once more from the neck, completed the turn, and dropped my head. Relieved and finally relaxing, I was able to drift back to sleep.

Later, with my sleeper still zipped tight, I got feverishly warm. My sack had turned into an incubator. Sweat steamed my body. I rolled on my back, kicking and flailing, but I could not break out. I let out a scream. Then another one.

Mother opened the door, saw my anguish, and rushed to help. She unzipped the sack. My arms were free. I felt my fear diminish and a shroud of steam move away from my body. Mother wiped my forehead and comforted me with understanding. Then she rested her hand on my shoulder and stayed with me. Reassured, I was able once more to go back to sleep, this time until morning.

Mother never zipped that sleeper to the top again.

She only pulled it up to my waist or so and always left my arms free.

In old age my mother could not move her arms. She couldn't brush her own teeth. Her mind reverted to the regions of childhood. If I mentioned Forada, she said, "Yes."

"Do you remember Forada, Mother?"

"Yes, I went to school there."

"And Maple Lake?"

"I was born there." She smiled at the reminiscence, and I smiled with her.

Then I reminded her, "Mother, it's me, Don." Her eyes looked ahead, empty. She remembered nothing beyond those earliest days.

"It's me, your son."

"Oh."

"It's your son Don."

"Oh, thank you."

I would hold her hand for a minute or two and then I had to leave, my sadness too difficult to bear; the blank incomprehension, crushing.

Other times, there was nonsense. "The car. No, I can't help it. Go ahead now. Tomorrow." Some days she saw things no one else saw. "Over there. By the window."

"Where, Mother?"

"He's very tall. Ask him now." She seemed certain.

This went on for years. Unbearably slow, painful years. And then she lost even the ability to talk. Dad got her up each morning, dressed her, and set her in her chair. Days upon days she sat there, mouth hanging open, sleeping or staring into the vacant air. A home health aide brought her food and spooned it into her mouth as if she were a baby.

One day she turned her mouth away from the food as the aide was feeding her. The aide tried again, hoping to direct something between her lips, much like a mother feeding her reluctant child. Mother clamped her lips and twisted her head. The health aide kept trying. Mother moved one way and then the other and tightened her jaw. Once more the aide tried to lever the food in. Mother refused. The aide paused, then tried again, still without success. Bits of food dropped from Mother's lips.

"Don't force her to eat," I said to the aide, suggesting that her efforts were now enough. I tried to say it gently. I knew that Mother was caught in a cocoon of death and did not want to go on that way. *I hope I don't die like my mother died,* she had said in her younger days. Senility, they called it, then. She was now undergoing the same relentless deterioration. I could think of nothing to do except let her refuse food if she wished. Her mind was gone, but I was quite sure that her behavior was now intentional. Letting her not eat and therefore starve seemed like the only way I could do something for her. I could at least understand and accept her wishes.

"Don't force her," I repeated to myself, quietly, to weigh the gravity of my words. Then my mind prayed to unseen forces: "Can't she go gracefully? There is nothing graceful about this. Take her soon." I felt uneasy asking for the death of my mother.

Father entered the room and said Mother had to eat or she

would die. I couldn't find the words to tell him, yes, she would die . . . and it was the right thing. I reminded him that his own father did not eat in the last days of his life, but he doubted it. He did not take in my words, think about them, discuss them. For him the controlling thought was . . . Mother had to live. They continued to feed her for many months.

Shortly before she died Mother visited me, perhaps in a dream, although it was so real, so vivid, I felt awake. It was during that vacant daydreaming time at dawn. Maybe I was awake. My eyes were closed and I was reliving a time in Cub Scouts. Mother was our den mother. She was teaching us to play ball—showing us first base, second base, third base—batter, pitcher—three outs to an inning, just as she had done once at Eastman Park in St. Cloud. I took my turn at bat. Mother was pitching. She arched an easy underhand throw right over the plate, even with my belly button. I smashed a grounder between first and second base.

"Run," Mother said, so I ran to first base. Nobody fielded the ball. "Keep running," she said. The ball rolled into the outfield, so I ran around second base and on to third. "Keep running," Mother said. "Go home." I touched third base and headed home. Someone fielded the ball, but it was too late. "It's a home run! It's a home run!" Mother shouted. I wasn't so sure. I had made it home, of course, but it was just a grounder. "It's a home run because nobody touched it," Mother said. "Otherwise it's an error." I realized, then, that it was all right to rejoice in my hit, that it was indeed a home run, in my imagination now, just like it was that earlier time. Mother wasn't just saying so; it was a real home run.

I knew Mother was with me during that surreal moment because I became conscious of an elevating joy. Somehow, through some supernatural medium, she had spoken to me. She was telling me that it was OK she was going to die. Together, at that moment, we were both very, very happy. I got out of bed, washed, and joined my wife at breakfast. "Mother came to me just this morning," I said. "She spoke to me. I'm sure of it."

Within a week Mother died.

Summer Days

WHEN I WAS A LITTLE KID it was fun to get up in the morning, at least in the summertime. Awakened by the daylight, I would hop out of bed, tear off my pajamas, pull on my underpants, put on pants and a shirt, and run downstairs, too young to feel the need to brush my teeth, wash my face, or comb my hair. I would eat breakfast quickly and then go outside for a run through the damp grass in bare feet. Mother would still be sleeping.

A hedge separated our house from the Salaskis' house to the north. There I found butterflies and caterpillars, which I caught and put in a jar with holes in the cover to show Mother later. Then I noticed bees. Maybe I should catch them too, but *no*, I told myself; I'd been warned of their sting. They flew to the hollyhocks along the north wall of our house and dipped in and out of the yellow and pink flowers. I followed them and put my finger into a flower; it was sticky with yellow powder. So that's what the bees were after, I learned. But I was young and had no need to watch their unending work, so I looked for new interests. I went to the sandbox to push around sand and cool my hands and feet in the moist depths.

Soon my younger brother would join me, and we'd climb

the Chinese elm growing out of the sandbox. It was short by adult standards but tall enough for us to feel adventure, and it was safe. If we fell we would land in the sand. Like monkeys, we clung to branches as we moved about, and as we grew bolder, we climbed as high as we could and then declared that we could see Third Street, half a block away. We never fell. Sometimes we would divide up the tree and call certain branches rooms. Bob would have his rooms and I mine, a playroom, a bedroom, a bathroom. I told Bob to stay out of my room, and he said I should stay out of his.

Other days we went to the garden, glanced at Mother's flowers in front, and followed the path down the middle in search of nature's snacks: grab some lettuce; pull a fresh radish if enough pulp showed; try for a carrot but usually end up tearing off the top; eat an onion if we could stand the sting.

Sweet peas were the easiest to get. They climbed up the little trellis built just for them along the outside border. With our fingernails we cracked the shells, then ate the little green balls. Farther back we found pole beans, potatoes, and tomatoes. Walking among these, we were near the back of our lot. A fence and multicolored hollyhocks marked the border. Altogether this little patch of ground—meant to help feed our family—was a visual and delectable Eden. But even Eden had its serpents, and in the thick foliage of beans and tomatoes we found mosquitoes. They fed on our flesh until, defeated, we moved on.

For another treat Bob and I picked rhubarb, which grew behind the garage. The stalks were chewy and gave off slightly sour juices. I could gnaw and savor one for half an hour. When the rhubarb leaves were extra large we each picked a mighty

Don and Bob in the side yard, St. Cloud, ca. 1944. We were sometimes mistaken for twins.

one and carried it around, triumphantly, as though we had accomplished something big, like cutting down a tree, or we treated it like an umbrella and shielded our little bodies from the sun.

More snacks grew on the south side of the house. The vines growing up the chimney gave off tendrils. I picked them and chewed them for their slight grapefruit taste. A mouthful could last awhile, like gum. And, finally, for dessert, a honey-suckle bush blossomed by the front gate. Here I picked flowers, bit off the bottoms, and showed Bob how to suck out the nectar. It took a few to get a buildup of taste, but the bees had shown that success takes work. When satisfied with nature's gifts, Bob and I would lie in the grass and let it tickle our skin. An ant might crawl up my ear. In the sky, clouds looked back and seemed to wink.

One summer my father and older brother Richard built a chicken coop and placed it in the rhubarb patch. Then Dad bought home about a dozen chickens. I found it fun to watch them dip to take a drink, then tilt back and work the water down with rhythmic swallows. Each day they seemed to grow in size and add more feathers. By summer's end the chickens were full-grown, and Dad said it was time to butcher them. Mother boiled some water and Dad got out a stump. Frank Schroeder, our neighbor to the south, came over with his hatchet. As Dad held a chicken over the stump, Frank chopped off its head. Dad then released the chicken's body and let it run. It took a half dozen quick steps and then lost its balance and fell. To my amazement, it got up and tried to run again, then fell again, and then tried to rise once more but reeled around instead in death throes while blood throbbed out of its neck. I watched from behind a tree, afraid the ghost-driven bird would head toward me. And as I watched, I realized what Mother meant when she sometimes told me I ran around like a chicken with its head cut off. Finally, the chicken rolled on its back, gave a few weak kicks in the air, and died. Mother picked it up and dipped it in boiling water to remove the feathers.

Sometimes, for summer adventure Bob and I would climb into the top of the garage and walk the planks on the second level. This was exciting for a while but not much fun for it was very dirty up there, the dust having billowed in from our dirt driveway. There were very few finished driveways in our town. On windy days, when her laundry was hung out to dry, Mother would complain about dirt in the air. But Bob and I could dig holes in that dirt for a game of marbles, and Yvonne could trace a design for hopscotch. Inside the garage, in the front corner, our family kept tin cans to be recycled in the war effort. It was my job to stomp the cans flat. I made sure I wore shoes for that.

To the south the Schroeders' house sat close to our lot line. In back of the house was a shed, and farther back an unused chicken coop. There was no garage because the Schroeders had no car, although a relative living with them kept one parked in the street. A short fence connected their house to the shed. I learned to reach through the fence gate, push up on the hook, and quietly enter the Schroeders' yard and hang around their back steps until someone noticed me. Then I would ask if Lois could come out and play. Lois was my girlfriend, everyone said, and they were right. She was pretty and fun to be with. I planned to marry her when I grew up and together we would live on a farm, plans that developed from the simple pleasures we had during those summer days in her backyard. She would offer me a drink from their outdoor pump. It took the two of us, one to pump and the other to drink. I liked a girl who shared like that.

If Lois couldn't play I would watch her father work. He was a mail carrier, so he would be home by midafternoon and have time for jobs around the house. I'd watch him spade compost in his garden and leave nice even rows of soft black soil. I'd admire his work and watch for worms at the same time. Once Lois's father taught me how to putty windows without saying a word. I watched him cut the glass, then fit it in a frame, then push the metal points that secured the glass, and finally bevel a smooth layer of glaze along each edge. Artwork, I thought.

I remember one summer day in particular, August 15, 1945. I was not quite eight years old. Mr. Schroeder borrowed his brother's car and took Lois, me, my brother Bob, and a few other even younger neighborhood kids downtown. "The Japs surrendered," he said. "The war is over." When we turned onto St. Germain Street I was amazed at the ruckus, cars jamming the streets, horns blowing just for the joy of it. Mr. Schroeder parked the car, gave us each a nickel, and told us to stay on the block; then he went into a bar filled with exuberant, celebrating people. We youngsters wandered up and down the street and marveled at the happiness we saw everywhere, too young to really understand. I had known about one woman in town who had five banners in her windows, signifying five family members in military service. I understood the simple meaning then, but only now can I imagine her relief when the war finally ended. Flags seemed to be everywhere on St. Germain Street. I used my nickel to buy a flag from a street vendor.

Two hours later, Mr. Schroeder drove us home. The mothers in the neighborhood were waiting for him as he pulled up; they wondered where their children had been. One of them gave Mr. Schroeder a look that told him he had been irresponsible. We kids didn't think so. There was no serious danger; there was simply too much overflowing joy. Mr. Schroeder had given himself and us a way to remember one of the most important days of the twentieth century.

Wartime shortages ended shortly thereafter. For adults this meant unrationed food and fuel. For me it meant bubble gum, something new on the market. I stood in line at Carver's Grocery and bought two sticks for fifteen cents, an awfully high price. Soon after that it dropped to a penny apiece.

Many summer evenings, Lois, her older sister Mary, my sister, Yvonne, brother Bob, neighbor Skippy Hanson, and I would play "kick the can" immediately after supper, or after dishes if we had to do them. If we knew a game was waiting we did dishes very quickly. Our driveway was the principal gathering place. I loved the game, and guess everyone did, with its strategies for hiding to avoid getting caught and daring dashes for goal. At dusk, mosquito-bitten, but genuinely happy and tired, we were called in for bed.

Then summer would end. It began to get dark after supper. During winter it was harder to get out of bed. Mornings were dark except for the hallway light my father had turned on. The room was cold, very cold. Father had stoked the furnace, and heat was rising to the radiators but had not yet filled the room. Told to get up, Bob and I pressed our bodies and our clothes to the radiator. We shivered and dressed for school, but we wished we were in bed where it was warm or that summer could stay forever.

Danger

OUR HOUSE HAD THE NORMAL modern features of a 1929 structure, electricity, central heat, bathroom and kitchen plumbing, but there was a gas burner in the basement that was used to heat extra water for our Saturday night baths. It had to be lit manually with stick matches. When evening set in, my older brother would be sent downstairs to ignite it. My younger brother, Bob, and I followed and watched and of course begged to blow the matches out. That's how we learned about fire.

I was about five years old and Bob four when we were left in the care of Yvonne for a short while one afternoon. She was busy with something or other, so Bob and I decided we had a nice opportunity to play with fire. We went down into the basement, got out a few matches, and lit them one at a time to watch the flames dance and burn low to our fingers. This was fun, but in time not quite fun enough, so we decided to build a little campfire. We arranged matches in a triangular teepee on the concrete floor, then scratched one on a rough part of the floor and set the pile afire. The flame advanced slowly, then suddenly *WHOOSH, WHOOSH*, individual matches flared up and began to scare us. The fire seemed to threaten

Our St. Cloud home, before vines grew up the chimney.

our house. I knew it was time for action but couldn't decide quite what to do. Maybe go to the washtubs and draw water, but that would take time, since I had to get a pail and something to stand on. While doing that, I thought, the fire could spread out of control. Better to just watch it.

Bob ruminated less in times of crisis and on this occasion responded immediately in the most natural, obvious way. Without embarrassment or bravado he pulled out his little shooter and peed directly into the fire. The flames hissed out. Jeebers, I was relieved—although not in the sense he was. I wanted to tell everybody how smart and heroic he'd been. But the wiser course was to clear up the mess as best we could and hope nobody would ever discover it, so that's what we did instead.

A day later, Father noticed smudges on the floor, got the story out of us, and lectured us on the danger we had created. "Never play with matches," he said. "Never!" Mother added emphasis. "You could burn the house down. Then what?"

First Love

I HAD A VERY EARLY LOVE AFFAIR. Not Lois, another one. It still has an emotional hold on me that I cannot shake. Nor can I re-create the conditions that bring it back and enjoy it again. I can relive it in my mind and rekindle its delight only in memory. I miss it, sometimes quite a lot.

Since my father worked in a lumberyard, one of his jobs was to go out to farms and take measurements of buildings. Often he would stop at home first, pick up Bob and me, and take us along. We were quite young when this started, since I remember that we wailed in self-pity once when it appeared he had stopped at home and then left without us. He came back and told us to quit making such noise, that he hadn't left for a farm. But when the opportunity did come, he didn't forget us. I believe he took us along so that he might enjoy his sons, and at the same time give Mother a rest. But, to me, it was always a trip into my imagination, an exciting, bounding, youthful love affair.

I knew the Old MacDonald song about farm animals and I'd read, or had read to me, storybooks about visiting "Grandma's house" on the farm. I may have even seen movies in farm settings by then. Always, farms seemed so interesting and different from our house and yard in the city. When my father took us with him I got to see up close what was in my imagination. He talked business, while my brother and I explored.

It was just like the stories. There were pig barns, with piglets climbing around sows, each in their own compartment. Each compartment had a door to the yard outside. It looked like a nice comfortable arrangement for a pig. "But don't put your hand in with a nursing sow," a farmer told me. "She might get angry and snap." The pigs were black with a white strip around the middle. "Poland China," Dad told me when I asked, and I learned the breed. But I wondered at the geographic strangeness of that name.

We went into the chicken coops, and I learned to tell the roosters from the hens by their long combs. It was fun to look in the nests to see if there were eggs, although we had to watch carefully where we stepped. Most farmers left the chicken coop door open so the chickens could wander all over the farmyard in search of bugs and grain. I envied their boundless freedom. In town, chickens were kept in pens, somewhat like Bob and me, who were often told by Mother to stay in our yard. I learned that farm chickens returned to their coops every night without being called. Their habits came from the sun.

Sometimes there were sheep. Mostly they were just fun to look at or to touch if we could, and I noticed a film on my hand when I stroked their fleece. "It helps keep them dry when it rains," Dad said. Bob and I chased a few sheep across the farmyard once and thought they looked funny when they ran; their back legs hopped, like rabbits.

Always, we wandered into the barn. Most had a similar layout, but still we found them interesting. Toward the front there was a stall for horses. Once, a pair of huge draft horses was tethered there, resting. "Good for fieldwork," Dad commented and mentioned that riding horses were much thinner. "Why don't they lie down?" I asked. "No need to," the farmer said. "They can sleep standing up." I looked at him in disbelief. "Yup," he said, and then I believed him.

Bob and I looked farther into the barn and saw stanchions for cows. It was midday and the cows were out to pasture, but this time one was still at its stall, perhaps a new mother or one that was sick. I squatted low to examine her milking parts and wondered if I could make them work. The cow turned and looked, and I could see her eyes say, *What are you looking at?* Embarrassed, I moved on. In the back of the barn we found a pen for calves. A farm boy showed me once that you can put your finger in a calf's mouth and it will suck so hard it almost pulls it off. Another pen, boarded to the ceiling, held the bull. We didn't dare get close to that.

Then Bob and I looked in the hayloft while Dad and the farmer talked. I imagined a boy could climb and slide and have fun up there. He could also hide way in back and no one would know where he was. I tried to climb up the stack but couldn't get a toehold. Bob found another way to climb up and had a long bouncing slide, just like in the storybooks.

We looked in the granary, the corncrib, the icehouse. On other farms, we slipped through the barbwire fence and walked in the pasture to see where the cow paths led. Once I found a stile just like in the English nursery rhymes. I tried to climb it, but the steps were too high. Bob followed me wherever I went, but I didn't pay much attention to him. I was exploring, and every direction in the farmyard seemed to lead to new, exciting activities.

Now I'm old. I still visit farms when I get the opportunity. I'm always secretly hoping to find a "grandma" farm. Instead, I find near factories with modern machinery and animals in confinement. I cannot identify with these animals, stunted as they are in lifestyle and personality, housed in gray metal sheds. They don't graze in pastures. Their feed is measured and rationed; they stand in yards around the barn.

Many farmers have no livestock. Some don't have a garden. They raise endless fields of corn and soybeans. For more production and easy fieldwork, sloughs have been drained and the creeks they fed are now dry. Farmer and wife usually work in town. The farms of my memory are gone.

Even the farms of my dreams were not real, I've found. My wife, who spent some time on an uncle's farm when she was young, says that her remembrance is of flies and manure and an outhouse. A friend of mine who grew up on a farm says he hated getting up at five in the morning to milk cows. Others have told me they thought farmwork was grueling. They wanted to move to town, participate in after-school activities, live an easier life. To them the cities were exciting. These people make sense, but they must not have experienced the thrill I did. Young girls read about princes and castles and fall in love. I had read about and visited farms and formed a love affair with them, an emotional hold I may never shake.

Trip to Canada

"WE'RE GOING TO WINNIPEG. The whole family," Dad said, as he unfolded two maps, one of Minnesota and the other of Canada, on the dining room table. He was talking to whoever in the house might be listening. I left the house of cards I was building on the living room rug, pulled up a chair, and leaned in right next to Dad's elbow, eager to see and learn more.

Then he spoke quietly, just for me.

"See? Here's where we are, St. Cloud. And here's the Mississippi." His finger traced a sweeping line upward from the center of the state in the form of a backward question mark. I knew a little of this from geography lessons in school, but not everything. I liked it when he talked and showed with his finger. We would think together and his finger looked long and the nail was clean and smooth. Some people had dirty nails, but if they were friendly, I didn't care. Dad's were clean. I decided I liked clean better.

"We'll go to Lake Itasca. Right here. That's where the Mississippi starts. You can walk across the river there."

"No."

"Yes, it's just a little stream there. You can walk across it. It gets bigger as it goes.

"Then we'll go up to Bemidji," and he pointed out the bold print of Bemidji on the map. "You'll see a big statue of Paul Bunyan and his blue ox."

I was anxious to see Paul. I'd read about him in story-books. He seemed as big as our house.

"Then we'll go to Grand Forks over here on the North Dakota border. We'll probably stay overnight there." He hesitated to think about that for a moment, then pulled out a Lucky Strike, tamped it on the table, and lit it, never looking up from the map. I liked the smell of burning tobacco and I liked the plume of smoke, straight for a few inches and then winding into a corkscrew shape. When he held the cigarette near me, I ran my finger through the smoke and disturbed the pattern; but, always, it returned to form.

"Bring me an ashtray from the living room," he said quietly. I ran and got one. It was fun. He was planning and I was helping.

"From Grand Forks we'll go straight north to Winnipeg. That's in Canada." He placed the other map on top and showed me how the road went off the top of one and onto the bottom of the other. "Here's Winnipeg. Winnipeg's a big city. Some of the people speak French—in a section called Saint Boniface. We'll drive around and visit it."

"Your grandfather Morris was French," Mother said to me from the kitchen. "His father came down from Quebec."

"We'll spend a couple nights in Winnipeg," Dad continued, ignoring Mother's family history. "Then we'll go east to Kenora. It's supposed to be very pretty." He pointed out the word Kenora on the top edge of a sprawling patch of blue.

"This is Lake of the Woods. It runs from northern Minnesota way up into Canada. Kenora's on the edge of the lake."

It looked nice even on the map, a land of long roads between towns, a land of blue lakes and green forests. Lake of the Woods ran off in many directions. I wondered what it would be like to see it in person. Such a pretty name, I thought; there must be woods all over. And I imagined a pretty little town down along the water named Kenora.

"Then we'll go across to Port Arthur* and Fort William, way over here on Lake Superior. And see here? There's Kakabeka Falls. We'll stop to see that."

"Kakabeka. That's a funny word."

"I suppose it's an Indian name," Dad said.

"Then we'll come down along Lake Superior." He moved his finger. "They call this the North Shore. We'll stop and see Gooseberry Falls." His finger stopped. My eyes stopped with it. "See here?" I looked close and made out the letters. "You'll like Gooseberry Falls. It's a triple waterfall."

"You'll have to be careful on a waterfall," Mother fretted from the kitchen. "Those rocks are awfully slippery."

"Then we'll go to Duluth to see the ore boats and a bridge that lifts up and down so the boats can go under," Dad continued. I thought about what he said.

"How does a bridge lift up and down?"

"It's controlled mechanically. You'll see."

"Then we swing up into the Iron Range. There's a huge open pit mine in Hibbing. See? Here's Hibbing."

"What's that mean, an open pit mine?"

---

*Now combined into Thunder Bay.

"A big hole in the earth. Bigger than any you've ever seen.

"Then we'll come home. The whole thing should take about a week." In my mind I'd already taken an exciting trip. I couldn't wait to get started, me and Dad, and, oh yes, the rest of the family.

When the day came we stopped at Grandma Hall's to say good-bye. "Take the Lincoln," she said. "It's bigger." So we unpacked Dad's Plymouth and took Grandpa's 1941 Lincoln. Mother and Dad sat in front. Jerry sat on Mother's lap. The other four of us sat in back, arguing for position. We drove the route Dad had outlined, and I liked everything about it because he had prepared me so well.

When we got to Kenora we stopped and walked around the town. There were colorful banners and Canadian and British flags all over and Lake of the Woods reached to the edge of town and looked just beautiful. My older brother Richard said he was going to come back someday when he got older because he liked it so much.

Then we drove east of Kenora and saw empty houses and farm buildings. Dad said they were abandoned.

"What's *abandoned* mean?" I asked.

"It means the owners have left them. They've given them up."

"Then are they free for whoever wants them?" I asked.

"Yes," he said, "although I suppose you'd have to pay back taxes."

"How much are those?"

"I don't know."

If Dad didn't know, there was nothing more to ask. But I

told myself that I should remember those farms, save some money for taxes, and then come back when I got older and live for free. And maybe bring Lois. The two of us could make it work. And when I wasn't busy I would visit Richard in Kenora.

I also decided that if I had kids I would be a dad like mine, who spoke to younger people in a way they could understand.

Fourth Grade

WE DREW FROM A LOTTERY to exchange Valentine gifts in Sister Annice's fourth-grade class, and I thought the heavens opened just for me when I pulled out a slip of paper that said simply: Patty Henkemeyer. I had noticed her exceptional cuteness already in the second grade. She hadn't changed—black curly hair; white teeth evenly spaced; cherry lips; pinafore dresses. She was still in first place in my informal rankings. Now that I drew her name she would have to pay attention to me at least during that moment when she opened my gift. And what if she looked me in the eyes and smiled. Jeez, I shoved my hands in my pockets and stared at my shoes over the embarrassment of it.

I decided the right gift would be a candy bar, a full nickel bar, not some cheap penny Tootsie Roll or gumball. I wanted Patty to know I thought highly of her, and I wanted her to think the same of me. It would be a Baby Ruth candy bar, nuts covered with chocolate. I liked Baby Ruths, and simple logic told me she would like one as well.

Four days before Valentine's Day I bought the special candy bar. Nobody else needed to know what I was doing, especially my mother, who would pass some kind of judgment on my actions, so there was the problem of keeping it in a safe, secret place. I decided to carry it in my pants pocket, the place where I carried my own candy. That should work. It was February, so it wouldn't melt. I carried it throughout the school day, even out to the playground for recess where we played tackle football on the sandy grounds near Lake George. I favored it when I fell and it never broke or got crushed.

Sister Annice knew how to dramatize events like Valentine's Day. When the time came, she had each person individually present his or her gift. I rather shyly gave mine to Patty. She seemed pleased. I was pleased. No cheap gift from me. Then Sister had each student individually open his or her gift so everyone could share in the pleasure of it. First the girls, then the boys. I was anxious for Patty to open mine; she would like it so much, I was sure. She might not know I had protected it close to my body for a few days, but she would know I cared because of the expense and the rich chocolate flavor. In fact, maybe it was too expensive. Maybe she would think I cared too much.

Soon it was Patty's turn. Gently she opened the wrapper. Sand fell out. She lifted the bar and it was coated with playground sand. "Ugh" she said. "What is this?" She was polite enough not to throw it in the wastebasket immediately; she set it down and looked at it and I suppose contemplated why someone would give *this* to her. What was his message anyway?

There was no message. There was only embarrassment and no words.

Sister Annice seemed to understand what had happened and suggested I buy another gift. I did, but it was quite anticlimactic. By then I hoped Patty would forget the whole episode and especially who was responsible for her gift. But, in case she didn't, I did not look at her for the rest of the school year.

And that was OK, because I really liked Marlene Reiter. Patty was one of those opportunities for stardom; but if I had to settle down for a long life together, it would have been with Marlene. My earlier girlfriend, Lois, was a year ahead of me in school, so I was now noticing other possibilities. Marlene was new to the school, a transfer student from Kansas, the Sunflower State. I thought the image fit nicely. Her cheerful face was runner-up to Patty's glowing looks, but she ranked higher in overall appeal because she was so smart. I didn't have a full scale rating system in the fourth grade—just general considerations—but I liked smart and cute together. Marlene met the standard. She also laughed easily; that helped, too.

Sister Annice divided the class into two teams for competitive achievement: the Lions and the Tigers. Marlene and I were Lions. David Heim was a Tiger. David was very quick at math. I enjoyed being matched against him and usually it was a standoff, but since Marlene was on our team and she was smart in so many other things our team usually won. These contests were held in the front of the class, so I got to observe Marlene and her skills. She knew where Burma, Siam, and French West Africa were on the map. She knew how to spell *aspiration* and *confusion* without mixing up the similar sounds at the end. She knew when Minnesota became a state and other important dates. I liked that brainpower and I paid attention to her . . . but she didn't seem to notice me. She seemed to concentrate on her schoolwork.

I observed that Marlene favored her right leg. She walked on her toes on the right side but came down fully on her left. Apparently it was a condition caused by a childhood injury. Some might have called it a limp; I considered it a dainty feminine gait.

One day Sister called Marlene to the front of the class to receive a paper, which took only a moment, and then she started to return to her seat in the back of the room. I was seated halfway down the aisle, and she would be passing right by me. When she got close I stuck out my foot, apparently to slow her down so that she could pay attention to me. It was an impulse. I wasn't in the habit of doing this; it just seemed to happen on its own, like when the front of a young boy's pants sticks out at the wrong time. Marlene tripped and fell headlong down the aisle. She was embarrassed. She looked back in search of the obstacle that caused her to fall and seemed to examine the base of my desk, but by then my feet were in their proper place. Apparently unhurt, she arose and continued on her way. I felt terrible. I was too young to know enough to apologize. Besides, how could I explain something I didn't even understand? I said nothing.

Fourth grade was good to me in every other way—I enjoyed the learning contests and the bashful flirtations and I thought Sister Annice was a truly fine teacher—and maybe it was even good to me in my failings. I didn't know it then, but I would learn that, over time, mistakes seem less important and I would also learn as I got older that everyone has embarrassments.

Baseball

AT THE AGE OF TEN I contracted pneumonia and was placed in a hospital for ten days. Every four hours, nurses shot penicillin in my butt, and soon my little rump looked like it had measles, or so I was told by chuckling observers. I couldn't see it much and I didn't especially like people commenting on my butt . . . *then*. I was thinking of other things, like getting healthy and playing baseball.

My parents would visit every day and bring things to play with or magazines to read. One day, during a visit, I told my dad I wanted to be like Walker Cooper. I had read about him in a magazine.

"Walker Cooper? Why?" he asked, and I explained that Walker Cooper was a major league catcher who made only one error all season, and that's what I wanted to do. I might have picked Stan Musial, Ted Williams, Bob Feller, Joe DiMaggio, Lou Boudreaux, or Hal Newhouser, all headline names at the time, but Walker's record of near perfection seemed like something I should try for.

Boys gravitated to natural positions on the ball field. A tall fellow would play first base; a quick one, shortstop; a smaller one, second base; a strong arm, third base. Nobody wanted to play right field because that meant you had no skills. The fact that Babe Ruth played right field about fifteen years earlier didn't occur to us, I suppose, because home runs were beyond our ability at the time. I decided I was catcher material. Catchers participated in every play. Catchers called the pitches. They had to be thinkers. They had to be reliable. I would be a catcher like Walker Cooper. Although he has since dissolved into forgotten history, Walker Cooper's singular memorable season was an inspiration to me.

"Well, I agree," Dad said. "That's a good choice," after I explained my desire to be like Walker Cooper.

Out of the hospital and able to run again, I played ball on the crude homemade diamonds near our house. There was one by the granite company sheds and another by the railroad tracks. You could spot them by their backstops made of 2 x 6 lumber and chicken wire, and the worn paths from base to base. Aside from that, they were simply empty pieces of ground. The area around home plate was bare dirt. If it rained the night before, puddles stood until midafternoon in the hollows created by kids scraping for position in the batter's box. A rag, a piece of cardboard, or somebody's mitt could serve as a base. There was no pitcher's mound; instead, there was a hole the size of a shoe sole, which the pitcher had to toe before throwing. Sometimes home plate would be a piece of lumber, cut the right size, sitting on the ground. When it got hit by a pitch or a bat or somebody's foot, as it did about every other play, the plate would splay out of place and the catcher or batter would reposition it. If there was no home plate, an opposing player's mitt would do while his team was at bat.

The catcher also called balls and strikes because he had the best view, although there certainly were arguments about his judgment, and maybe his intelligence.

Grass was left uncut. This was no problem in the infield as it was trampled to stubble. In the outfield, though, one could easily lose a ball hit somewhere in the long grass, but an out-fielder might get lucky and pick up one lost from a previous game and surprise a runner thinking he should easily make an extra base.

We young players learned how to spit on those fields. There were two basic styles: squirt it easily between your teeth, or blow a little gob through a hole in your lips. After a little practice, it came easily. A more advanced technique was the *ppffffttt* for tobacco juice. I dribbled down my chin on the first few tries but then, by learning to push with my tongue, became quite good at it. Spitting was so *major league*. Just the sight of a homemade field, any field, if we were driving around town, would stir my energy and make me want to jump from the car, run onto the field, spit, thump my mitt, and imagine throwing a runner out.

"I found a catcher's mitt I want to buy," I told my dad when I was twelve. "I've checked all the stores in town. I can buy it for six-fifty at Hugh Morris. It's nine dollars at Pap's Sporting Goods. The same mitt, near as I can tell. I also checked Powell Hardware, Ladner's, and Firestone, and they didn't have any-thing as good." I always had to get permission for big expen-ditures like that, since Dad paid for them. If he said no, there was no purchase, although I would try to wear him down with pleading.

This time he said, "It sounds like you've done a good job comparing. Go ahead and buy it." Usually when he said this he reached for his billfold. This time he didn't.

"But what about the money?"

"You've got money." He smiled. "If it's something you really want, go ahead and buy it."

He had never answered like that before. I had to think. I did have a paper route, but Mother managed those earnings, made sure I collected from everybody, made sure I counted the money correctly, and then made sure I saved about 90 percent, leaving me just a little for occasional treats. I realized he must be telling me to spend my savings. I asked Mother about the money, and she agreed that buying the mitt seemed like a good idea. I felt *exalted*. My parents trusted me to make a good decision. It was the first time they treated me like an adult, and it was such a surprise. I bought the mitt and became a real catcher.

My brother Bob and I played catch daily in our driveway. He was the pitcher and I the catcher, although some days we would reverse it just for practice. The garage was our backstop, which worked pretty well because the doors were always open. But really wild pitches cracked the wood siding alongside the doors. Home from work and inspecting the yard and surroundings, Dad would look toward the garage and notice a new crack. He would grimace but not say anything. He liked our playing ball.

One summer morning Bob flung a pitch over my head and through the window of the garage door, which was slightly ajar. We figured that was a pretty serious casualty and stopped playing for a while. One of us would have to tell Dad when he got home.

After lunch we felt the need to play again, but this time in the street. I got to hit fly balls to Bob. He would catch or shag them, and then in turn we would switch roles. Early in the game I managed to hit one squarely and loft it clear to the corner, well over Bob's head. It felt good. However, a car was coming down the side street and by some celestial precision reached the corner just as my ball was landing, which it did, right on the driver's windshield. I didn't feel good anymore. I knew I was supposed to own up to my behavior, but I didn't know how to deal with some irate adult whose face was probably smashed. I ran in the house, got my mother, and told her what happened. She said, "Come on," and together we went down to the corner to check on the accident. The driver was a kindly old man. When he got out of the car we could see he was uninjured. His windshield was surely smashed, but not him.

"I'm sorry, are you hurt?" Mother said. I stood nearby.

"No."

"My husband works up the street at the lumberyard. He'll make sure it gets fixed. I'll call him."

"Thank you. What's your name?"

"Hall. *His* name is Marce Hall."

"Oh, I know Marce. I'll talk to him. Everything will be OK."

The kindly man accepted her assurances and drove on toward the lumberyard.

Bob and I decided to leave the street and take our ball game back up to the driveway, only this time in a simple game of catch. I was the pitcher, he the catcher. After a few pitches I picked up a stone, as players do, and threw it aside, just an easy sideways toss, and it went right through Schroeder's nearby basement window. It didn't bounce off; it made a bullet hole straight through the glass. How could that happen? I thought; it was such a soft throw. We'd have to tell Dad about this, too. Three windows in one day. Bob and I stopped playing ball for good that day.

Dad came home for supper. "I heard about the windshield," he told Mother as she was slicing Spam. "I told him to get it fixed and I'd take care of it."

I was listening, gauging his mood. He stepped into the bathroom to rinse his face and hands, then came back into the kitchen, wiping his hands.

"There's a couple more," I said.

"A couple more . . . what? Windows?"

"Yes. One in the garage and one in Schroeder's basement."

"Really. We better go see." We went outside, and I showed him the damage. Bob joined us. "We were just playing catch," Bob said.

"Well, keep the garage doors open," Dad said, in an even voice, "and the windows won't break."

"I know. I guess we just forgot," I said.

Then he went over to tell Mr. Schroeder that he'd fix his basement window.

"How'd it go?" Mother asked when Dad returned.

"Frank said he would fix it. He's got time. 'Well, the least

I could do is bring the glass,' I told him. He's an awfully good neighbor."

In another year I got better at catching, and pretty soon Bobby Kosel, a neighbor from the next block, two years my senior and a very good athlete, came over to practice pitching. His fastball I could handle, also his knuckler, which didn't move much at that time, but his curveball was a problem. More than once it hit the dirt in front of me and bounced and struck me in the area—ahem—where it hurts so much on a man. I didn't own any protective equipment. When struck in that sensitive area I would hop around on one foot and then the other, double over, writhing, and grimace for a minute or two. Then I'd straighten up, take a deep breath, and resume catching. I hated every time he threw a curveball, although they weren't all so crippling. Catching, I learned, was not a job for sissies.

In the eighth grade at St. Mary's we had a good team, and we played the other Catholic schools in town. Mark Lippsmeyer and I took turns catching. We had a face mask, but no chest protector or shin guards, and somehow didn't get injured. (We also played football with no equipment, no helmets, in the eighth grade and didn't get injured.) Our team was undefeated. We had the advantage of being the largest school in the league.

In summer league we played against some older players, and I remember a game against Roger Collins, a strikeout ace. The game was scoreless until the last inning. Then an opposing runner got on base and after a couple of outs advanced to third. The next batter hit a ground ball, and the runner headed for home. I stepped up to guard the plate, received the throw in time, and stooped to make the tag. It was an easy out ... except that he slid into me and I dropped the ball. That is, as an inexperienced player, I forgot to squeeze the ball. We lost 1–0. I had read about Mickey Owen and how he dropped a third strike and the Dodgers lost the 1941 World Series. Sportswriters called Mickey Owen a "goat" for the rest of his life. Why a goat? Short for scapegoat, I guess. But everyone knew it was a term of derision. I knew I was a "goat" that day, and I worried that nobody would ever forget, that I would be like Mickey Owen, the major league catcher who dropped the ball, not Walker Cooper, the player of near perfection.

As I got older I wore proper equipment. That made the job even harder. Shin pads have buckles just behind the knee. A catcher has to get in a crouch for every pitch and after a few innings the buckles began to grind on the back of the knees. If a pitcher walks two or three batters an inning, exasperation sets in. Chasing wild pitches and passed balls becomes fatiguing. Batters stir up dust. On hot days catching becomes a sweaty, grubby job. I began to experiment at infield or outfield positions, looking for easier work. Batting was always fun, so it was important to find a position and stay in the game. Senior year in high school I switched to intramural softball. I hit first in the lineup, played left field, and got lots of action. We won the championship. It was simple competition, but fun.

After high school, George Mische, a hometown friend, organized a team for Sunday afternoon "town ball." He wanted me to catch again. We played other pickup teams in neighboring small towns. Pretty ragged games, most of them were, and with tiring innings for me behind the plate. But success at bat and an occasional stolen base made it fun. And drinking beer in the taverns afterward made it great fun. One afternoon we were scheduled for a doubleheader against Waite Park. In the first game the opposing pitcher had a no-hitter going until the last inning. I was the last batter up, and I stroked a clean single over second base. In the next game George had me bat fourth in the lineup, the place for power hitters, a place of respect. I was no power hitter, but I appreciated the gesture. We celebrated with beer that afternoon, too.

In later years, when I was off at college, my youngest brother traded away my catcher's mitt, not realizing what it meant to me. It meant as much as my first kiss, maybe more. But like that kiss, it was gone and all I had were memories, which, when I thought about it, was about all Walker Cooper had, too.

Entertainment

KIDS TODAY ASK what we did before television.

I never thought of it in time, but I should have asked my dad what he did for entertainment on Friday nights or Sunday afternoons in the early 1900s, before movies. Most likely he played cards. I'm guessing at that, because his mother played cards, and whenever there were two or three or four gathered at her house she brought out the cards for a game of cribbage, skat, hearts, whist, pinochle, or canasta. The folding card table was always up. It was almost as much a part of the living room furniture as the davenport. She would entice anyone, including us grandchildren, into a game. She loved cards. My mother was similar, and so were other mothers. Card tables stood in their living rooms, too. Men played cards at the beer halls and clubs. They also played at home. Sometimes whole families would spend a Sunday playing poker for pennies. More intellectual people played bridge. Cards must have been the principal entertainment of my parents' generation.

I visited one of my father's cousins once when she was in a rest home. An upbeat and cheerful woman in earlier times, she had by then suffered a small stroke and it affected her strength. "I can't even holdt tah cardts anymore," she said in

Germanic English. Tears filled her eyes. I could think of nothing to console her. No cards, no life, for this fun-loving woman.
She died about six months later, probably of despondence.

We young people played cards. We also liked to listen to
the radio. Sunday nights as we drove home from a relative's
house Dad would tune in *Amos and Andy*, which featured
white guys impersonating blacks, and *Charlie McCarthy*, the
sassy puppet of ventriloquist Edgar Bergen. These were half-
hour situation comedies. Other times, we kids listened to Red
Skelton as he impersonated different characters, or to Dick
Contino, who kept winning first place with his accordion on
The Horace Heidt Talent Show, or to *The Life of Riley, Judy
Canova*, and other favorites. I also occasionally listened to
Minneapolis Laker basketball games, and in my mind saw
Slater Martin bring the ball up the floor, pass to Pollard or
Mikkelson, who in turn passed to Mikan for a turnaround
hook shot and an easy two points. Virtually every male in the
state listened to the Minnesota Gopher football games on
Saturday afternoon. In 1949 the Gopher team was a power-
house. I knew the names of all the players, but in listening got
so excited that I made Bob come out in the front yard to play
tackle before the game was over. I could read about the details
of the game and the final score in the peach-colored sports
section of the Minneapolis paper the next day.

But our principal entertainment, both boys' and girls', I believe,
was the movies. Our town had a big Paramount theater six
blocks from our house and, at an early age, my sister, Yvonne,
took Bob and me to see the movies on Sunday afternoons.
Like every child I loved *Bambi*, *Snow White*, and *Pinocchio*. As

an adult I went to see *Pinocchio* again and discovered it was just as heartwarming as the first time.

Cartoons, sometimes more than one, were shown before the movies. I grew to like Bugs Bunny and Daffy Duck the best, although I must have been older by the time I appreciated them because there was generally a psychological twist to their antics.

Newsreels also preceded movies. I remember an announcer describing victories in World War II as bombers blazed across the screen. The crescendo of noise aroused patriotic fervor. Everyone clapped spontaneously; we were proud of our country at war. I don't remember seeing concentration camps. Perhaps they were shown and I was too young to grasp their importance. Previews, advertisements, and sometimes short "specials" also played before the movie began. Because of this, I sometimes had to ask Yvonne, "Are we seeing the movie yet?"

A real treat was a double feature, that is, two movies for the price of one. Sometimes it was a surprise; we learned of it only when the first movie ended. We had to watch both, of course, as the second one was a gift. That meant four hours at the theater on a Sunday afternoon, something my parents seemed not to mind. Occasionally we'd stay just to see the same movie twice, the second time free, of course. A movie cost twelve cents then; ten cents for the movie and two cents for tax. Think of that, a 20 percent tax.

As I grew older, movie entertainment got slightly more sophisticated, but not by much: Esther Williams swimming to music, a couple falling in love in *State Fair*, Tarzan of the jungle, Red Skelton being foolish, and manic Jerry Lewis. I enjoyed Pa Kettle, the lazy, cornpone philosopher, and his frazzled wife, who tried to keep the kids under control while the house and farm fell apart. *Cheaper by the Dozen* celebrated a family of twelve kids. William Bendix played Babe Ruth, the baseball hero who had recently died. We also saw simple religious movies like *Going My Way* with Bing Crosby as a priest and Jennifer Jones as the girl from Lourdes who had visions in *The Song of Bernadette*.

A small theater in town, the Hayes, showed mostly cowboy movies. Roy Rogers presented glitter. Gene Autry, amiability. Red Ryder and Hopalong Cassidy seemed more real. The Lone Ranger fought crime. For a year or two, my buddies and I attended those. We were haughty by then and laughed through their obvious plots. Pauly Condon gave a running commentary of advice to the actors. Stuff like, "Hey, watch out behind you," or "She doesn't love you, don't believe her." Or for clarification to the general audience when a scene ended in a loving embrace: "He's trying to feel her up."

The Eastman theater showed reruns. I followed the ads in the paper closely in case I missed something the first time around, or so I could see something especially likable a second time.

As I reached high school age I began to like musicals. Kathryn Grayson in *Showboat* made me gape, breathlessly. She sang in the clouds and carried my emotions there as well. I raptured over her face and demure manner. Even today if I see a woman with luminous red lips, like hers, shaped like a kiss, I stare, probably inappropriately, and I wonder if she sings. And there was Mario Lanza, a hero in my youth. Not everybody's hero, but certainly one of mine. His may still be the finest tenor voice ever to come out of America. Unrefined, the critics said, but God Almighty, what power and glorious range, and sweetness. Masculine, too. Just right to a young lad. When he sang out his love to a girl, you knew he meant it. I was sure if I could sing like that I could win any girl I wanted. Lanza starred in *The Great Caruso* and other movies.

When I was in high school, a new drive-in theater was built west of town. My parents weren't much interested in movies and I couldn't drive at the time, so my first opportunity came when an older friend of a friend got the family car and took a gang of boys to the drive-in. I sort of invited myself along. I was a little uncomfortable being with older fellows I didn't know too well. Also, I hadn't told my parents, and I hoped I wouldn't be out too late. But what the hell, I kept my problems to myself and tried to be cool. I learned how an outdoor theater worked. There was one big screen, but a speaker for each car to hang inside the driver's window. We saw Gordon MacRae singing and dancing in *The Daughter of Rosie O'Grady*, a pleasing but forgettable movie.

Midway through the movie, I had to go to the bathroom. I got out of the car, walked around and found the right building, made my stop, and then tried to retrace my steps. Very soon every car looked the same. I had forgotten to make any note of the car I arrived in. I walked up one row and down the next. I tried peeking in windows, but that was risky, very risky, since somebody might be "necking," or *more*, inside. I kept walking around, hoping I'd somehow recognize the car. Finally I gave up.

My pride badly damaged, I went to the projection booth and told the operator I was lost. "OK," he said and he asked my name and the name of my driver. I told him. Then I realized that the whole theater was going to learn of my ridiculous plight. The operator waited for an appropriate break in the action on the screen and then he announced over the public address system at great volume so everybody could hear: "PHIL SCHMID. PHIL SCHMID, PLEASE COME TO THE PROJECTION BOOTH. DON HALL IS LOST."

The guys didn't tease me like I thought they would. Nor did my parents learn where I was that night.

By the time I was seventeen we had television in our house, and the movies—"films," as they're now pretentiously called in Hollywood—became less and less important. Now, only the old Paramount theater remains standing, having been restored recently with fresh paint and rich velvet and brass appointments. It looks better than I remember. It's available for "special occasions." The Eastman and Hayes theaters are gone, replaced by progress, I guess. And a strip mall with a multiscreen theater now announces your choice of movies, afternoon or evening, where the marquee of the old outdoor theater in the early dark of evening used to shout in bright lights "NOW PLAYING . . ." and I couldn't wait to see it.

Travel

*Don and Bob see President Truman, General Eisenhower,
Ted Williams, and Joe DiMaggio*

IN OUR FAMILY, travel was considered educational. Dad was
proud of the excursions he planned, and Mother used them
to teach us things. Besides the trip to Winnipeg, there was a
trip to see the natural wonders of the Black Hills and Yellow-
stone, another to see Glacier National Park, where my sister,
Yvonne, was working for a summer, and still another to see
the skyscrapers of Chicago. Mother and Dad called them vacations, but they weren't very relaxing. The real purpose was
to see and learn things, and that was true for our parents as
well as us five children. We would pack in the car and drive
off, Dad trying to make time and Mother telling him to "quit
zooming" so she could point out things along the way.

Most Sundays in the summer we took a short trip to
Grandpa Hall's cottage on Grand Lake, fourteen miles from
our house in St. Cloud. Those were simple excursions back
in time and therefore educational in a special way for me. At
the cottage there was no plumbing, electricity, or refrigera-
tion, and only a fireplace for heat. I liked having to pump for
a drink of water and read by a kerosene lamp—and when
the urge came, use the outhouse or, at night, the chamber
pot. Degradable garbage was simply buried in a hole in the

ground. And there were farms nearby. When we stopped at one to buy ice for cooling our food, I learned that the blocks will stay frozen throughout the summer if they are buried under sawdust in a shed built just for that purpose.

Mother's interest in travel started early and without much assistance. In high school, there was the walk she took with friends to the Canadian border. In college, she and her friends walked seventy miles from St. Cloud to Minneapolis, with an overnight stop at Elk River. Dad knew of her plans, so he and Lloyd Tenvoorde, a buddy whose family had the local Ford dealership, got a car and drove off to find them. They spotted the girls beside the road and rolled down the windows to wave and tease and offer a ride. The girls were determined to walk.

While working in Idaho, Mother and some of the other teachers acquired a car and took it for rides on Sunday afternoons, often in "gumbo," the wet Idaho clay roads. On one occasion, they seemed to run out of gas while driving up a hill. They fretted about what to do until one of the women realized that gravity kept the fuel from flowing into the engine. So they turned the car around, backed up the hill, and everything worked fine.

Dad's first serious trip may have been from a barn loft. At a young age, he got the idea that he could fly with an umbrella. It should work, he thought, because he planned to use a very large delivery-wagon umbrella. Why not? Hadn't Orville and Wilbur Wright been doing strange experiments around the same time? He jumped up and out and expected to float, but the umbrella snapped back, and he went straight down into a manure pile. In old age he once drew upon this experience to summarize his life in metaphor. "I jumped into a manure pile and lived," he said. Others have, too, only he really did get his shoes stinking.

When he was eighteen, Dad and his family took a trip they talked about for the rest of their lives. Ten of them—the two oldest boys stayed behind to handle the lumber business—took two cars to visit Grandfather's sister, a nun at a convent in Louisville, Kentucky. On the way down they drove through Chicago and when they got on the Outer Drive, Grandma's hat blew off, never to be seen again. This was memorable, for in St. Cloud you could always park your car someplace and retrieve your hat. But not in the busy city of Chicago. Perhaps it was she who named it the Windy City.

Because of the primitive roads it took a week to get to Louisville. When they were finished visiting, Grandma insisted they go home by way of St. Louis so she could attend Mass at the newly constructed cathedral. She chose well. I've seen it and believe it ranks among the most beautiful buildings in America. The interior walls are covered with richly detailed mosaic, something you might expect to see in India. It is a gorgeous building. But for Grandma it was equally important to attend Mass.

From St. Louis they started out for home. Before long a tire went flat, something that happened often in the early days of the automobile. They used "the spare" to get to the next town, hoping they'd find a gas station that sold tires. That worked just fine, but Grandpa was short of cash and he offered to pay for the new tire by writing a check. The attendant hesitated. "Taking a check from a stranger so far from home could be risky," he said. But after thinking for a minute, he decided to accept the check anyway. "Anyone traveling in two cars with that much family must be good for it," he said. The story became family lore on how important it is to be creditworthy.

A year or two later Dad left home. Without a word to anyone, he and his buddy Lloyd Tenvoorde went to the woods in northern Minnesota for adventure and money. They worked in a lumber camp. Lloyd's assignment was to peel potatoes, while Dad was ordered to cut trees. He told of getting up one morning when it was 20 below zero and being led by an Indian to the trees that needed cutting. By noon he was in his shirtsleeves, warm from the sweat of work. Dad didn't mind the work, but after ten days of peeling potatoes Lloyd was disgusted. "Let's get out of here," he said, and the two of them decided to leave for home. They walked out of camp and caught a train to Duluth and then home. That was enough wanderlust for Dad; he never felt the urge to leave St. Cloud again, except for vacations.

My special educational opportunity came in the summer of 1950. The Boy Scouts were sponsoring a national jamboree at Valley Forge, Pennsylvania. At twelve, I was the youngest age allowed, but Mother thought both Bob and I should go. "The older one will look after the younger," she told the authorities. "You can bend the rules a little. They're both the same size. They'll be fine."

"I think it's the opportunity of a lifetime," Dad said.

"You will learn so much history," Mother told us, "and you'll meet scouts from all over. Everyone is supposed to bring souvenirs to trade. You can bring little samples of St. Cloud polished granite. It will be an opening for conversation."

It sounded exciting to Bob and me, and we both agreed we'd like to go. We could use our paper route money to pay for expenses. So we signed up, as did six other scouts from town and our special scoutmaster for the occasion, Al Frank.

After elaborate preparations, including packing the granite souvenirs, we were ready to go. We even had our picture in the *St. Cloud Times*. The scouting authorities arranged for a special train, possibly brought out of retirement, just for our trip. It was powered by a slow, coal-driven locomotive. When we boarded, the train was already half full with scouts from upstate Minnesota, but Bob and I found some empty window seats and settled in for the long ride. The train worked its way to Minneapolis and then St Paul, picking up scouts at various stops along the way. Then it went south along the Mississippi River, picking up more scouts until it was full. I watched the river grow large at Lake Pepin, and then spread out into backwater among the islands near Winona. I noticed bluffs high on either side of the broad valley. They looked like places where Indians once camped and sent up smoke offerings to the Great Spirit. I was taking in nature like a good scout. At Lacrosse, the train stopped again. Although unsure just when it might start again, two scouts took a chance and got off the train. Quickly, they came back with candy bars, which they offered to sell for a dime apiece.

"That's too much. They only cost a nickel," someone said.

"So what. Do you want one or not?" came the reply.

"Not me," the boy said.

And not me, I thought to myself, and don't you buy one either, I said to Bob. It's not worth it.

Still, a few boys agreed to pay the price. I was intrigued, but a little repelled by the profiteering—especially from Boy Scouts.

The train headed east. At dusk we lowered the seats. The seat bottoms slid forward and the backs dropped down so that an individual seat became flat like a bed. As everyone did this, two platforms formed down either side of the aisle. Someone opened a window wide to let in the night air. Once we stretched out, bodies intruded on each other's space. We lay down anyway—two, three, four abreast—and tried to find a comfortable position for sleeping. As one squirmed, the other adjusted. Soon our toiletries and other things held close were scattered about. By morning everything was in disarray. One kid got annoyed at another, so he threw a jacket at him, missed, and it flew out the open window. It was funny to those of us watching. The jacket was gone forever, we thought.

But the jacket was important, the owner realized, and he ran to the end of the car and pulled a cord that signaled the engineer to stop the train. I watched, wondering if it would work. So did everyone else. Then we noticed the train beginning to slow down. Is it really stopping for a jacket? And then the train came to a halt. The kid jumped off. I worried we might leave him behind, that the engineer was really stopping for something else. But the boy ran down the track, picked up his jacket, ran back, and jumped on the train. The engineer must have been watching, for he started the train again. I was amazed. Trains were supposed to be time-bound carriers of freight and people. They stopped for nothing but emergencies. They even had "cowcatchers" in the front of the engine to push livestock out of the way. Here we stopped for a kid's jacket. The others on our car must have thought the same thing. We looked at each other and then began to laugh at the absurdity of it. Then someone started to celebrate the kid as a hero for his bravery. "He stopped the train," the boy said. "One little kid stopped this locomotive and all the cars." With that, everyone was proud to know him. "You're great," said one boy. "Saved your jacket," said another, beaming with admiration.

When the train got to the Appalachians it went through tunnels. The first time through our entire car filled with sooty smoke. It took us awhile to realize what was happening. The tunnels would fill with the engine's chimney smoke, and if we didn't close the windows, it billowed into the train. From then on we learned to close the windows quickly whenever we entered a tunnel, but always someone would forget and we'd get another dose of pollution, slowly, until we again realized what was wrong. It was dark in the tunnel, so we couldn't see to close the windows.

After three days we reached Valley Forge. Scouts were coming in from all over the United States and foreign countries. Forty-seven thousand of them. We were to camp out like General Washington's soldiers on the rolling plain of Valley Forge, a national park. It was called a "crusade to strengthen the arm of liberty."

A few years earlier the country had won the war against Germany and Japan. But then Soviet communism pushed

Valley Forge, Pennsylvania, 1950: 47,000 Boy Scouts.

into Central Europe and was now threatening Western Europe, our allies. Communists had also seized power in China. The country positioned itself for another war, if necessary, this time against communism. Without realizing it, we scouts were being prepared to uphold the "the arm of liberty." Even though we didn't pay attention to international politics, we knew we might someday be called to be soldiers. But we didn't think about it then, not that summer in Valley Forge. We were too young to be thinking about the future.

Scoutmaster Frank helped us set up camp and get ready for the jamboree. We were to sleep in three-man tents and cook over charcoal stoves. When the work was done that first night and we had finished eating, I was exhausted and very much ready for bed. So were the others. At dusk, as I lay on my back awaiting slumber, a bugler played taps. I knew the words: "Day is done, gone the sun . . ." Then another bugler in a unit down the way played taps also. Then another . . . and another . . . and another. The notes resounded throughout the valley in solemn echo, as though General Washington were calling us to sleep. I drifted off easily that night, feeling safe and lucky.

The next day Bob and I walked around to meet other scouts, learn about things, and have experiences like we were supposed to. It was an education. Scouts from Montana knew how to crack a bullwhip. One showed me how, but it took a number of tries to get the hang of it. They had Mohawk haircuts, and I thought I might try one when I got home, if Mother wouldn't get too mad. Texans had horned toads to trade. When I offered one a piece of granite in exchange, he said, "No, not fair." Some scouts wore coonskin caps, others wore Indian regalia. Scouts from West Virginia brought coal to trade. Who wanted that? Granite was better. From Florida came oranges; from Hawaii, leis. I wouldn't trade for an orange; you eat it and it's gone. Nor for a ring of flowers. The Canadians played bagpipes.

That night we attended the official opening in a great outdoor natural amphitheater. It took almost an hour just to file into our places. President Harry S. Truman was invited to speak. Here we were, face to face—although at great distance—with the leader of our country, a great honor, we were told. He would speak about world events. We sat on the ground and listened. It was an important talk, I'm sure, but I remember none of it. What I do remember is that he had to stop in the middle and ask the audience to quit taking pictures because the glare of flashbulbs made it difficult for him to read his speech.

"Ha, ha, ha," laughed one of the boys next to me. "Old Harry Ass Truman, with thick glasses, can't read his speech. Ha, ha, ha."

"Ya, what an old fogey," I said. "He should tell us jokes or something." Aside from that, I was polite and listened, but comprehended very little.

On the Fourth of July we gathered in the great amphitheater again. This time General Eisenhower gave us his view about world politics, and then he had us pledge allegiance to the flag. Again we were aware of the great honor to be present and again it was boring—until the end, that is, when there was a great fireworks. The best I'd ever seen. Stuff flying through the air and bursting over our heads, and at the same time there were stationary fireworks on the stage, red, white and blue, in the form of a flag, and then it changed to look like a waterfall. Very impressive. It went on for half an hour.

There were other pageants on other evenings. One reenacted the American Revolution. At the final one we all lit candles and dedicated ourselves to God, country, and brotherhood.

After the first day of walking the grounds and seeing other scouts, Bob and I and the others in our little unit grew weary of culture. Instead, we looked behind our campsite and discovered the Schuylkill River. It was about as big as the Sauk River back in St. Cloud, shoulder-deep at the most. We rolled up our pant legs and waded in and caught crayfish. Then we went in deeper, ignoring the fact that our pants were getting wet. Someone started a mud fight. Soon everyone joined in.

We threw mud and splashed and dunked each other if we could. Then we swam in deeper water to clean up. In the days that followed our little group skipped the planned events and choose to play in the river instead. Once he checked it out, Scoutmaster Frank didn't mind, but he did tell us he thought we should be taking advantage of the once-in-a-lifetime activities. To us, however, the river was more fun. Conversation with strangers was awkward.

One day we walked upstream to a farm. There I saw a cow that looked very sick, with guts hanging out of its backside. The farmer said it was "afterbirth." I didn't quite understand; it seemed like an awful thing happening, whatever it was. He inquired where we came from and then told us to be careful of the river water, since it was polluted with animal manure. We ignored his suggestion. It couldn't hurt much. We had already played in the water and no one got sick. After about four days of water games, I did worry some that we weren't doing what we were supposed to do, and that a lifetime opportunity was slipping away. I also felt some responsibility to make sure Bob was doing what he was supposed to do. But Bob and I and the others in our group were having fun. I decided it was too hard for boys to give up fun and do what they were supposed to, even when they were Boy Scouts.

After a week of mostly pageants at night and mud fights in the day, we loaded up and moved on by train as scheduled for New York City. But first there was a brief stop in Philadelphia to see the Liberty Bell and Independence Hall. I got to put my finger into the crack of the famous bell, but for only a moment, as the crowd behind me pressed to keep moving.

Then we went on to New York, where we were going to see the Yankees play the Boston Red Sox at Yankee Stadium, the famous "house that Ruth built." More than that, a postgame visit had been arranged with Joe DiMaggio. Our scoutmaster brought along a leather gun case, which was to be a gift for the great Yankee center fielder. Whether Joe had a gun or not I don't know, but we assumed he would appreciate the gift. When we arrived for the game we found our reserved seats along the left field line—too far from home plate to really see balls and strikes—but close enough to see left fielder Ted Williams when he got into position. I watched in admiration as he spit into his mitt and bent over ready to play. And when he wasn't in the field, DiMaggio was, and then I studied him. In the seventh inning a messenger came looking for us and told us that we couldn't all see Joe DiMaggio after the game as planned; there would simply be too many. We would have to pick one delegate. I very much wanted to be chosen. It would be better than seeing President Truman or General Eisenhower, I thought. If I couldn't be chosen, then my brother Bob should be the one. I would experience the excitement through him.

"Decide among yourselves," our scoutmaster said, "but decide quickly." We left our seats and gathered at the rear of the seating deck to try and come up with a decision.

"Bob should be the one," I said. "He's the youngest." Secretly I hoped he would then suggest me and tell the others that I was most qualified because I knew a lot about baseball. But he didn't.

"I'd like to go," said one fellow.

"So would I," said I, realizing I had to speak for myself.

"Me, too."

"Why not me?"

"And me," said Bob.

"I have an idea," said the biggest scout in the group. "Let's pick Rolly. He's a little guy. Let's let him be big once." And then everyone seemed to agree.

"Ya, Rolly. He should be the one."

"Everyone likes Rolly."

"That will settle it."

"OK, then it's Rolly," and various scouts nodded in agreement.

I was envious, but the conclusion seemed fair and I was happy for Rolly. I liked him, too. If it couldn't be Bob or me, then Rolly was best.

In the ninth inning our scoutmaster and Rolly went down to meet the great DiMaggio. When the game ended we had to stand around and wait for their return. They were back quickly.

"How did it go?" I begged Rolly, eager for any description. "What did he say about the gun case?"

"He wouldn't see us," Rolly reported. "A man told us he wasn't feeling well. We left the gun case." Now I felt bad for Rolly. He had won the personality contest but lost the prize. He was quite disappointed. As were we all.

"DiMaggio felt well enough to play the game," our scout-master said, and we caught the judgment in his tone.

While in New York we also went to the top of the Empire State Building—100 stories up—and took a boat trip around Manhattan. I suppose the boat trip was intended to be educational, but what I most remember is young boys jumping into the river from the banks of the New Jersey palisades—naked. The boat captain said they were wearing their cellophane suits.

Then we took the train home. This time it seemed a long and uneventful ride. After two and a half days we arrived at eight in the morning. Mother and Dad were at the station, smiling, happy to see us and very eager to hear about our trip. "How was it? What did you do? Did you see New York? Oh, look at your clothes, they're all wrinkled. Did you ever change?"

We tried to be gracious, Bob and I, but we had little to say and fell asleep in the car as Dad drove the short ride home. Mother emptied my bags to get at my dirty laundry; out fell the souvenir pieces of polished granite.

Lake George

IN MY FATHER'S DAY, I'm told, there were sloughs west of St. Cloud all the way out to Pleasant Lake, seven miles away. They drained into and formed Lake George near the center of town, which in turn drained out through a ravine to the Mississippi River. Lake George was far bigger than it is now, for it extended to the steps of St. Mary's School and over to the original Technical High School building, that is, maybe a third of a mile.

When I was young the sloughs were still west of town (in what's become the Crossroads shopping area), but the drainage bed from the west had been filled, paved with streets, and platted for houses. Lake George was a pond. And the outlet to the Mississippi was closed, also built over with houses, but you could still find a little evidence of the ravine in the terrain between the lake and the river.

The area in front of St. Mary's School had been filled with sand. This made a nice, soft playground, good for young boys playing tackle. On the far edge of the playground, sand was still being trucked in, further shrinking the lake. It was unloaded in individual piles, or dunes. My classmates and I called them "the hills." In the spring, snowmelt and groundwater would gather in the low spots between the hills and form little puddles that froze at night with half an inch of ice. We young boys, out for school recess, loved to run across that ice. The water beneath would bulge and dip; the ice would crackle and bend, but not break. We called it "rubber ice." After a number of runs, the ice looked like shattered windshield, but still it held. It seemed like nature's rules were suspended. In time, of course, under the heat of the day, the ice would give way and a youngster would plunge through up to his knees. And he would get appropriately disciplined when the teacher noticed his soaking shoes and pants. We knew the risks, of course, but that was the excitement. There was danger, and we were testing it.

The principal role for Lake George at the time was to provide winter skating. It was the right size for that. In January when the ice was a foot thick, a city truck scraped it clean of snow, then brushed it, and sometimes gave it a coat of water to create a fresh, smooth surface. I watched the work from my desk near the front windows of St. Mary's. After school, we boys played hockey on the fresh ice, and a few girls practiced figure skating. We used two lumps of snow to mark the goal. In the January cold, we'd play for half an hour and then head for the warming house to thaw out. This was a two-story brick building set along the east shore. It must have been framed with old railroad ties for it stunk of creosote, but it was warm. Upon entering, one could almost *see* heat radiating from the potbellied stove. My friends and I sat as close to that sweltering stove as we could and then, for entertainment, sprayed it with spit to listen to the sizzle of near-instant evaporation.

"Goddamn kids," muttered the custodian when he saw us,

and then clarified what he meant: "Cut that shit out." He didn't leave his chair in the corner of the room, however, until it was necessary to throw a couple more logs in the stove. Intense heat gushed into our faces as he opened the door, and we saw raging orange flames, an almost dizzying contrast to the icy wind out on the lake. My nose dripped from the thaw.

The bathroom, if you could call it that, was upstairs. I had to unlayer my clothing, of course, hold my mittens under my arm and then relieve myself in a metal trough that was meant as a drain but didn't empty. The smell of urine, mixed with the pervasive creosote odor, seemed to hold up the walls and press in on my clothing. I tried to hold my breath when I entered that room, but couldn't and invariably gasped a time or two and felt I had swallowed the foul mixture. I worried, lest my mittens drop in the yellow slag. The sink dribbled a few drops of water into a basin, brown with corrosion. It was a small victory to get out of that room healthy. Once outside and skating again I grabbed a handful of snow to wash my hands and breathed deeply to air out my lungs.

Still, I loved that warming house. I loved it in January for its heat and the few candy bars and pop available for sale, and in February for its ambience as it overflowed with boys and girls lacing up their skates on Friday and Saturday nights. By then the weather was comfortable outside. An adult played records in the upstairs window and broadcast the music over the lake. Floodlights illuminated the night. Everyone skated in a big circle, round and round, to the "Skater's Waltz" and other dreamy tunes.

Lake George and the warming house. Courtesy Stearns County Historical Society.

Girls would skate, hand in hand, two, three, four together, gliding as they do in figure skates. Boys skated alone or in packs, on hockey skates. Everyone was in winter clothes, so we boys searched the crowd for a cute face or slender legs. It was acceptable for a boy to come up beside a girl on the end of her row, take her hand, and hope she wouldn't skate too fast. I learned quickly that skaters moved faster on the outside than on the inside of the circle. I had weak ankles and it was hard to keep up when my skates bent out, not straight up like they're supposed to be. Girls didn't seem to have that trouble. They would stand erect and propel with ease. I was bent over like a hockey player, working my legs strenuously.

I'd grab a girl's hand and try hard to be graceful and romantic for a couple of turns around the circle. No conversation was necessary. Holding hands was exciting enough, even though I often didn't know with whom I was skating.

Pauly Condon talked about taking a girl or two and skating off to the edge of the lake near the piled snow called "the banks." It was darker there, away from the lights, and more conducive to mischief. He planned to accidentally fall and then pull the girl along and roll around to get a little feel. "Come on, Donny, let's go," he said one night as lots of cute faces glided by. We skated away and reached for the hands of a pair of girls, he on one side and I on the other. Pauly led the way, first in wider swings from the circle, then gradually out to the banks. The girls seemed to be enjoying it, although nobody spoke. When we were away from the bright lights, Pauly fell and pulled us all down. We rolled around on top of each other, with Pauly and me flailing around like we were out of control. I knew it was a bad thing to do, but I went for a feel, pretending it was accidental. Then I noticed that my female partner was wearing a sweater and a puffy jacket. It was impossible to tell the difference between layered clothing and sensuous flesh. This was a game of imagination, I realized; we weren't even close to the real thing. When they got their footing, the girls skated away.

I felt guilty over that act. I knew that girls were trained to call you an animal if you behaved like that. I had learned in school that improper sexual intentions were a mortal sin, and I would go to hell if I were to die without confessing my sin. But a sin is only mortal if you really intended to do it, the teachers had said. If your intentions are not set, then it is only a venial sin and not deserving of hell. I considered the whole experience and decided that in this case it was mostly Pauly's intention, not mine. I just happened to skate along. So, for me, it was just a venial sin. I did admit to enjoying it, though.

Mostly, we young boys just skated round and round as we were supposed to, and tried to connect with a pretty girl by grasping her hand, then sending and receiving love currents through two sets of mittens. Lake George was paradise those Friday and Saturday nights when I was starting to like girls. I didn't care about its history and which way it used to drain. That sheet of ice, along with the music, the lights, and the girls, was paradise in winter.

Catholic

IT IS DIFFICULT to overemphasize how intensely *Catholic* our life was during my youth in St. Cloud. When I hear about Muslims praying five times a day and fasting during Ramadan, or about Orthodox Jews keeping kosher, or about religious processions in Guatemala, or about prayer beads or icons or pilgrimages, I am reminded of our kind of Catholicism.

Our religion was filled with prescriptions on how to live. We were taught to protect ourselves from the amoral culture of the modern world and most particularly to avoid its temptations of the flesh, which we understood to mean sex. We were made to mind rules and behaviors under pain of sin. Certain transgressions, we were taught, if still with us at the time of death, brought eternal, everlasting, perpetual, relentless, excruciating suffering in hell. I didn't want my future condemned in such a way, nor did others I respected—my parents, grandparents, sister and brothers, friends at school, and everyone of importance around me—so most of us lived in fear of losing our souls, as it was put at the time.

There is a current joke that strikes at the truth of that period:

Somebody asks Hitler why he is in hell, and he says because he started a war in which fifty million people died.

So they ask Stalin why he is there, and he says he was responsible for the purge of thirty million.

They ask others, and finally somebody asks a simple Catholic why he is in hell. "Oh," he says, "because I missed Mass on Sunday."

To us it was no joke. We were taught, and we believed, that we would go to hell if we missed Mass on Sunday; or ate meat on Friday; or received communion without proper fasting; or swore in God's name; or entertained impure thoughts; or were sexual outside of marriage; or sexual with oneself; or even put oneself in the presence of temptation, like provocative movies or conversation or magazines with sexually alluring pictures; or looked upon another in an impure way.

There were other big sins, less intrusive in daily life—stealing, murder, suicide, euthanasia, abortion, divorce, idolatry, apostasy, and heresy. Fallen-away Catholics, people who had left the faith, were also living in sin.

The big test, at least for a young boy, was how to save his soul while going through the stirrings of puberty and adolescence and its sexual strains until safely settled into a proper marriage. We learned that in addition to procreation, one of the purposes of marriage was to "quiet concupiscence." Once married, of course, there was the issue of birth control. The only permissible method was the "rhythm method," which called for abstinence during fertile times. Sometimes it worked, and sometimes it didn't. There was no music with this rhythm; safe times were measured with the help of calendars, charts, and thermometers.

The way to remove a serious sin from one's soul was to go to a priest for confession, or absent that, say a prayer of perfect contrition with a promise never to commit the sin again. Even then it had to be confessed at the first opportunity. Weekly confession was considered a good thing, if not a necessity. If one died without confessing or being sincerely contrite about such a sin, one would be sent to hell—instantly and forever. If one received communion while bearing an unconfessed sin, one committed an even more serious sin, a sacrilege.

The sins were heavy enough, but there were also very strict rules about getting back into God's grace, which was done by receiving communion. Foremost among the rules was the requirement to fast from midnight until the time of communion the next day: no drink of water in the middle of the night, no breakfast, not even a crumb of bread, and no morning drink of water or juice, not even a drop.

"But, Father, what if I eat the seed from a crumb of bread by accident because I forgot I was fasting and then only thought about it later?" I asked one day in grade school. "You know how you sometimes pick up just a little seed and put it into your mouth?"

"Sorry, you can't go to communion once you realize you've eaten something," the priest answered.

"And what if you can't remember if you put that seed into your mouth or brushed it on the floor? You know, sometimes you might put one in your mouth and brush another on the floor and later you can't remember just what you did?"

"If in doubt, you can't go to communion. I'm sorry, but communion is very important. You must be perfect."

"But, Father, what about brushing my teeth?" another student asked. "I use water to brush my teeth."

"That's OK, just spit out all the water."

"But what if I don't get it all? What if I swallow just a little bit?"

"Sorry, you can't go to communion if you swallow water. Spit it out as best you can. If a little of the taste remains, that's OK. You can't help that."

"Father, what happens if I break the rule?"

"You have committed a mortal sin. That means if you die without forgiveness, you will go to hell. The rule is very important. It is so important that if you deliberately break it, you have committed a sacrilege, a direct slap to the face of God."

We were allowed to begin receiving communion at the age of seven, so we learned the rules initially at that time, and then kept asking questions over the years as our minds began to mull over the different circumstances. We wanted to get it right. All of us did. We were children learning how to save our souls.

I realized one day that since everyone in the congregation was bound by the same beliefs, it should be easy to surmise who in the church were sinners. Oh, there may have been other reasons why someone didn't go to communion—he or she may have gone to an earlier Mass (there was a limit on communion, once per day), or they may have been up late and

broken the fast. One couldn't be *sure* why someone didn't go
to communion, but if such a person passed it up repeatedly
there was room for judgment. That person must have committed a mortal sin and not yet confessed it—or worse, be
living in a state of continual unrepentance.

These thoughts gripped me powerfully one day as I attended Mass with my grade school class. I had been prepared
to receive communion when suddenly a great worry overcame
me: I might be violating the fast. I agonized over my condition while the priest consecrated the bread and wine. I really
wanted to receive communion, that is, enter into the state of
sanctifying grace, but in school Father had said that if I was
in doubt about my worthiness, I shouldn't. My mind argued
back and forth. It's OK. No, it isn't. I tried to concentrate as
the priest recited the Pater Noster, but I could not, there was
no putting the argument to rest. If I went to communion
without resolving the doubt, I would be committing a sacrilege. But if I did not go to communion everyone would think
I had committed a serious sin. I had prepared in every other
way; I was ready to go to communion. My brain throbbed
and I became flushed with worry. Then I decided that my
intentions were good; I would set my doubts aside and receive
communion. It was the right thing to do. But still I worried
and told myself, I can't be absolutely sure. God does not per-
mit excuses. God does not accept sloppy thinking. A stronger
argument one way or the other does not decide the question.
Either I'm ready or I'm not. The priest prayed the Agnus Dei,
then the Domine, Non Sum Dignus, asking God's mercy for
our sins. A server rang the altar bell signaling communion. It

was the time of great reverence in the Mass. Everyone bowed their heads to prepare for the sacred offering. I decided I would receive communion—God would understand—and when my turn came, I went forward and knelt at the railing. The priest approached, giving communion to the people near me. Suddenly, I was overcome with a final, overpowering surge of guilt. God will know and judge my actions if they are not pure. I am committing a sacrilege. If I die I am going to hell. So I arose and left the communion railing. I was sure everyone in the church noticed. Blushing deeply, I returned to my seat. I had turned my back on communion just as the priest was approaching. Surely everyone saw me. They would think I was carrying a mortal sin. But I felt I had no choice. God could see the doubt in my soul.

The next day I rushed to clear up this agonizing conflict by going to confession. "Bless me, Father . . ." I said, and told of a few small sins. "I disobeyed my parents two times. I told a small lie once." And then, "Father, I have a question."

"Yes, go ahead," he said.

"Father, is swallowing my spit breaking the communion fast? Is it the same as drinking water?"

"No," he said. "It can't be helped. There is no rule against that."

"Oh, thank you, Father. I just wanted to be sure."

He told me to say three Hail Marys as penance for my sins.

"Yes, Father," I said as I had been taught. "For these and all the sins of my past life, I am sorry. My Jesus, mercy."

"Go in peace," he told me.

The weight of hell lifted from me. I was in peace. I had been desperate to get free of my impossible interpretation of fast. I couldn't imagine how I could hold my saliva from midnight on through the next morning the next time I planned to receive communion. And if I could not go to communion, I would be stuck in the pews forever. The entire church would consider me a sinner. But this priest, this good Father, had released me from such a crushing scourge. He had put me back into a position to receive the grace of God.

As I grew older, there were other tensions. Adolescence brought the normal sexual desires, and always they were interrupted by the concern of damning my soul to hell for all eternity. Committing a sin was wrong, of course, but it was also wrong to put myself in "an occasion of sin." So, if I thought there might be dirty pictures in a magazine, I would be committing a sin simply by opening the cover, because I knew that before long, I would be enjoying the images inside. This made *National Geographic* a potential "occasion of sin," since I knew it might contain photographs of partially clothed native women. I looked at it anyway, and if I lingered too long on a page showing forbidden flesh, I confessed my sin later. It was a dangerous thing to do, though; I didn't want to die during the interim. Later, in confession, I would tell the priest, "I looked at impure pictures," or if there were no half-dressed women in that issue, "I *intended* to look at impure pictures. For these and all the sins of my past life, I am sorry. My Jesus, mercy." In class, our teachers, while discussing the persistence of temptations, gave us helpful guidance for dealing with them. Say ejaculations, they said. These were little spontaneous prayers like "Mary, mother of God, pray for me."

The word did not refer to body mechanics as it does now, or if it did, we were not aware of it.

I do not speak as a casual Catholic. I am as Catholic as someone who was born and raised in Italy is Italian. It is imprinted in my personality, just as being Italian is locked into the speech, gestures, and attitudes of someone from Italy. To remake this subconscious formation of my life would be almost impossible, and I would not like to try. There are some things I like about this imprint and would like to retain. But there is also much that has been changed or shed. Not just by me, but by many like me.

My wife, Marion, also from St. Cloud, and I both had nine years of Catholic grade school, including kindergarten, four years of Catholic high school, and four years of Catholic college. We received a fine education, but from a Catholic point of view. We were taught almost exclusively by nuns and ordained clergy. They always wore black and projected what we accepted as a special Catholic integrity. They would not cheat or lie, but, of course, they would be biased. We always assumed it was an acceptable tilt toward the more moral position and if "Father said" or "Sister said," it was so. They lived Catholicism even more than we did, and they were authorized to speak for the church.

Much of the unspoken influence in our lives was Catholic. Marion's father was an usher in church; her mother a devout, unquestioning believer who attended extra devotions at church. Marion had a second cousin who was a bishop. My father considered entering the priesthood in high school, had a brother who was a priest, and an aunt and a niece who were nuns. My mother converted to the Catholic religion upon marriage, so she was not immersed in the doctrine, but she supported the rules of the church concerning confession, fasting, attendance at Mass, and the extras like saying the rosary and performing acts of charity. Marion's name and my middle name came from saints. At confirmation we choose another saintly name for our own. We prayed to our guardian angels. In grade school Marion sang in the church choir. I was an altar boy. We received prayer books, rosaries, holy cards, and spiritual bouquets (prayers) for presents, and we treasured them. Boys were told to dress modestly, to wear a shirt in public; girls were given more explicit requirements, to be in no way provocative in dress or otherwise. I knew of a priest who threatened not to give communion to girls wearing lipstick. Almost all of our extracurricular activities, because the schools administered them, were under Catholic authority. This included sports, music, theater, and Boy and Girl Scouts.

A great deal of activity in our lives was specifically Catholic. We attended Latin Mass every morning in grade school and much of high school and college, went to benediction, said novenas, and prayed the rosary at special services. During Lent we made sacrifices: I would give up candy, or not listen to a favorite radio program, or skip movies; all adults had limitations on the size of their meals. Children and adults avoided meat on the appointed days, attended Lenten stations-of-the-cross services, and during Holy Week went to evening tenebrae. Pontifical High Mass on Easter Sunday lasted two hours.

On certain special days we participated in processions and

marched around town, praying for a good harvest or simply celebrating the Body of Christ. We prayed for more people to become priests and nuns; we prayed for the conversion of atheistic Russia; we prayed for the deceased, especially those in purgatory so that they might go to heaven; we prayed for ourselves so that we would get reduced time in purgatory.

We blessed ourselves with holy water in our homes. We built altars to Mary, the mother of Jesus. We bowed whenever we passed a church. We always addressed a priest or nun with respect. We called our bishop "Your Excellency." We joined organizations like Catholic Action and Young Christian Students; we pledged for the Legion of Decency. In sum, we were Catholic down to our underwear. No—more than that—we were Catholic to our heart, stomachs, and loins, especially the loins.

Our parents were members of mission societies, Christian Mothers, and the Knights of Columbus, all Catholic organizations. They were told not to join an organization like the Masons because it was considered anti-Catholic; same with the YMCA and the YWCA. Our parents supported the church financially, as they were commanded to under pain of sin, and helped pay for the Catholic schools. In addition, they were asked to support mission work in foreign lands.

The bishop was perhaps the most influential authority in our lives, not the mayor or some civic or business leader. He wrote letters of guidance that were read from the pulpit at Sunday Mass at least once a month. They were signed, "Sincerely yours in Christ." We accepted him as the earthly representative of the heavenly God. In the summer of 1950 the church declared a Marian year, after the mother of Jesus, and we were to pray the rosary with our neighbors in backyards after supper. I was a little apprehensive about being seen praying on our knees outside, but parents and neighbors organized and encouraged the activity, so, as children, it was quite clear we had to attend. Almost all of our neighbors were Catholic. Every night that summer we gathered in a semicircle like the children of Fatima and prayed before a statue of Mary. We saw it as a practice that would make us pleasing in the sight of God.

Every good Catholic family was expected to produce a priest or a nun. Some families, especially the rural ones, might have twelve to fifteen children and sometimes produce multiple priests and nuns.

Considering all, we may as well have lived in an Amish community. We were that controlled, that focused inward.

When I moved to Minneapolis as an adult I began to meet and talk to people other than Catholics. I remember a Methodist woman who was dating a friend of mine, who said she thought Catholics were superstitious. I was dumbstruck. We performed rituals that had meaning, I thought. Later I thought about the holy water, indulgence prayers, vigil lights, kissing the bishop's ring, confession, and I realized what she meant. I had never considered it that way before. I met Jewish people and Protestants and realized they were good people and surely must deserve salvation, even though we were taught only Catholics had the true faith. I was in my early twenties before I began to question these beliefs.

In 1959, Pope John XXIII, a beloved man who had long been concerned that much of the church's teaching was stuck in the Middle Ages, called for a Second Vatican Council to consider reform. This was four hundred years after the Protestant Reformation or, as Catholics called it, the Protestant Revolt. The church was catching up. The Vatican, we came to see, had been like a medieval kingdom intent on control of its members and protection from outside assault. Further, it had convinced itself that its decrees were divine. Once the council convened in 1962 and began to explore issues, outside influences and common sense took hold. Many fundamental beliefs were challenged. When Vatican II completed its work in 1965, priests began to quietly endorse birth control and no longer speak of mandatory Sunday Mass or Friday abstinence from meat. Matters of sin with implications for all eternity suddenly were no longer sins. For many Catholics this caused the whole construct of authority in the church to collapse. They no longer accepted anything. They no longer knew what to believe. They looked back at their previous beliefs incredulously.

I have changed. I no longer care about the dogmatic teachings of the church. Nevertheless, I am still a Catholic. I like some of the rituals like Christmas Mass, weddings and funerals, even the reminder on Ash Wednesday that our bodies will decompose. Who could not be comforted when someone dear is buried and the priest says, "Eternal rest give unto him, O Lord; and let perpetual light shine upon him. May his soul . . . rest in peace." In Latin, it was a mysterious ancient prayer: "Requiem aeternam dona eis, Domine: et lux perpetua luceat eis. Anima ejus . . . requiescant in pace." But that language has been set aside now. When I hear songs like "Ave Maria" and "Panis Angelicus" and "Stille Nacht" sung in a sacred setting, my soul quivers, every time. They are mystical, like a dream from my youth. I also appreciate the moral rectitude I was given. It has served me well more often than not. And I accept the social call of the church to help the poor. I am a cultural Catholic. I cannot be otherwise. Can an Italian be German?

Boarding School

SOMEHOW I THINK my father had a plan when he suggested I go to St. John's Preparatory School. I was fourteen years of age and would be leaving home. He had not sent my older brother and sister away to school, but he sent me, and then my two younger brothers. I would have a good study atmosphere and a better chance at success in sports and other extra-curricular activities, he said. The school was run by Benedictine monks and had only two hundred students, all boys. He himself had attended it when he was young, but that was because he was considering entering the priesthood. He didn't speak of it with loving praise; he spoke of it in practical terms. But I also heard him suggest once that it might be better for me to live on my own, to gain some independence. I took this to mean it would be better to be free of my mother's protective ways. He would never say such a thing directly, for he believed parents had to show a united front. I simply picked this up somehow from what he did say. Mother went along with the idea. She believed in pursuing opportunity.

Father believed in independence. "They have to learn for themselves," he said many times when someone did something dangerous, like using the railroad bridge to cross the

Mississippi River instead of walking a few extra blocks to the regular bridge.

"You'd think they'd know better. What if a train came?" Mother couldn't help but say.

"Well," he'd answer, "they just have to learn for themselves. You can't tell them." It was one of his basic beliefs, born of experience, I suppose, since he admitted once to crawling around on the lower bracing of the bridge when he was young. Just knowing he believed in the value of experience gave me the freedom to experiment and then forgive myself if I made an occasional stupid decision. He also didn't believe much in changing people by giving them handouts. "They have to get it for themselves or they don't appreciate it," he said. "If they want it bad enough, they can get it." He would cite examples of immigrants coming to this country and achieving success. Then he would add, "Even during the depression nobody starved to death." He was a self-reliant, small-town business-man. His father seemed the same. When Social Security was introduced, I'm told, Grandfather said he didn't need the government to take care of him. So in sending me away to school my father was teaching me self-reliance. Or more accurately, he was allowing me to be self-reliant. The price for this, as I remember, was $603 a year, for everything, paid by my parents.

I was excited about the possibility. We visited the campus on the grounds of St. John's University, eleven miles from St. Cloud, a year in advance and I saw a student sitting sideways in an open window during free time, looking unconcerned, two stories up. I wanted to do that rather than sit at my

St. John's campus; main quadrangle in the upper right.

cramped little desk at home. I wanted to be free to sit in a window if I felt like it. At home, if Mother saw me in such a position she would say, "Get out of there, you'll fall." I wanted to learn for myself. I envied the nonchalance of the young man sitting above us. When the St. John's athletic team played against our local high school, I paid attention to the players and their skills. I identified with them, not the home team. One of their basketball players was an American Indian. I had never met an Indian. What were they like? It would be interesting to meet one, I thought. There was also an occasional Negro student, another exotic element.

In the fall of 1951 I started school at St. John's.

At 6:30 A.M. a loud bell goes off. It blasts my ears and rattles me awake. I have been sleeping in a dorm room with about seventy other students, four stories up. Each of us has a bed and a stool. I close my eyes and roll over to sleep again but, before long, get a gentle nudge from the attending prefect. I sit up in bed, remove my pajamas, and put them under the pillow, then pull on my underwear, pants, and shoes. The student across from me has slept too long; he gets a knuckle rap on the head. I learn from that to be quicker out of bed in the future; I was lucky this time. I begin to straighten up my bed, as Mother taught me, but learn that it is not necessary. A hired man will be coming through to make them all. Hmmm, I think, I am in a position of privilege, but I feel slightly uncomfortable that a grown man will be doing this for me, a kid. I have been taught to serve my elders. But I take the easy way and try to fit in with the custom here. I leave the bed unmade.

From the dorm, I enter a large room where each of us has an individual locker for clothes. On the top shelf I keep socks, hankies, and toiletries, in the middle my few hanging clothes, and on the bottom a pile of clean underwear and a sack for dirty laundry. I take my toiletries and select a sink from among many in rows to wash my face and brush my teeth. Those who need to, shave. Freshened and dressed, we all go downstairs for seven o'clock Mass.

This takes place in an intimate, low-ceilinged chapel beneath the main church. As we enter from the rear, priests are saying mass quietly along various side altars. I kneel in a pew toward the front with the other freshmen, facing the main altar, and look upon the small bones of Saint Peregrine sealed in glass in the base of the altar. He died in Italy hundreds of years before. He is clothed in a simple gown and many jewels. I wonder about him. He died at my age, a boy martyr, flogged to death for being a Christian. Am I to die like him? No, times are different now. But surely his being here is intended to inspire me to be saintly like him, and to show that this is a place for reverence. The air is warm from the heat of candles and smells faintly of wax

Our celebrant enters for Mass. We bless ourselves and begin the prayers. "I will go in unto the altar of God. Unto God who gives joy to my youth." It is in English, not Latin, a progressive practice at the time. Quietly, we continue the prayers. They echo back, a monotone chant in the male register, mesmerizing. We could as easily be in a catacomb more than a thousand years earlier. But we are here praying in a comforting place, gathered with others, serenely, in conversation with God. "Holy, holy, holy, Lord God of hosts. Heaven and earth are full of Thy glory," we say as the priest is about to consecrate the bread. My body rests easy on knees and elbows and my spirit is at peace. We are silent as the priest prays sacred words. Communion follows. When Mass ends, the priest turns to face us and says. "Go in peace." "Thanks be

Relics of Saint Peregrin, 1953. Courtesy St. John's Abbey.

to God," we respond in reverence. It is a nice way to begin the day—although we are not free to do otherwise. We are learning the ways of the monks who run this school.

Breakfast follows at 7:30 in a large dining hall. Each of us has a regular place to sit and shares food in a set of four. Each has a cloth napkin, clean at the start of the week, and grimy with gravy, pudding, and other wipings by week's end. Classmates, working for tuition, serve the food. We learn soon that the food varies greatly in presentation and flavor. In the fall there is freshly harvested corn on the cob in nearly unlimited supply. I smear mine with butter and salt and eat four, five, six ears. The flavor is so good it is hard to stop eating. Once a week, whole-grained bread is served, still warm and soft, fresh from the ovens. Again we are treated to an unlimited supply. By the second week we eat bread ravenously whenever it is fresh, for we have learned that the bread will be cold and getting harder each day as the week goes on. When our foursome receives an occasional extra piece of meat or pie, we have strategies for deciding who gets the prize. One boy spits on the extra to make sure it is his. Another gets speared in the hand with a fork when he tries to make a claim. But mostly we are well behaved and learn to share by agreeing to throw fingers, calculate the total, and count off to see who wins. Once a week we get ice cream. Some students decide to sell theirs for a dime. Money is tight, so I seldom buy. But when a tablemate says, "You can have mine," I am dumbstruck. Giving away one's ice cream seems to me like giving away a date with a beautiful girl. I do not ask if he is being saintly or simply does not like the ice cream, although my mind wonders. I bypass sainthood and eat his ice cream. Although we are young and willing to eat almost anything, pork chops, baloney, "toilet trout," and fried potatoes have obviously been cooked in too much grease. We sample them, but send much back to the kitchen uneaten. My tablemates and I think the same potatoes are served day after day until, finally, in order to get fresh ones, we clean the bowl. Occasionally banana cream pie is served. My mouth waters. But when I taste it, the whipped cream is sour. I eat it anyway because it looks good.

After breakfast we go to our study hall, a large room filled with oversized desks fastened permanently to the floor. My desk holds all my books, pencils, paper, and private things like a nail clipper, gum, a mirror, and some personal letters. During my sophomore year it also holds a battery radio, which delivers the musical "hit parade" during our free time. But when the prefect is not paying attention, I sometimes play the radio very quietly during study hour. I lean my head close and listen to Kay Starr and Teresa Brewer sing about love. My eyes gaze in incomprehension at words in a textbook. Sweet music beats studying. I make up for these poor study habits by taking notes in class. Outside the study hall we have individual lockers where I keep a jacket, an overcoat, overshoes, and ice skates. Gym clothes are kept in still another locker in the gymnasium.

Classes start at eight o'clock and go until noon. So far there is no need to leave the building, a large brick quadrangle. The church is in one corner and everything else connects in a square around it. Sleep is on the top floor, eating in the basement, the other activities in between. Monastic quarters are on the opposite side of the quadrangle, behind signs forbidding entrance. I am not curious about life behind those doors. The monks have told us there is prayer, sleep, and study—and a little recreation like cigars, cards, and games of pool. We know their life is simple. "Ora et labora," their founder said, pray and work. Some of them are our teachers and our prefects. Others teach in the college, work on the grounds, or on weekends say Mass in neighboring parishes.

After lunch I am free until three o'clock. Everyone must get involved in at least one sport, the prefect says. We must do this for physical exercise, he explains, but hints that there is another reason. I think he wants us to use the showers in the gym since there are none for our use in the quadrangle. He seems to worry that a student uninterested in sports might go all winter without taking a shower. Football, basketball, volleyball, bowling, and softball are all available on an intramural basis. As the seasons come, I sign up for them all. The afternoon break is also used for varsity sports, music, ham radio, preparation for school plays, and working on the school newspaper. When there are no scheduled activities, or say, on a Saturday or Sunday, I find a friend and use the time to explore the woods, look in on the farm buildings, skate or toboggan in the winter, and swim or go boating in the spring. I come to realize I am living on twenty-five hundred acres of wilderness, agriculture, and civilized communal sharing. I come to see it as a blessing. It meets all my earlier, eager expectations.

In the late afternoon there are more classes and then a "study hall." Supper is at 6 P.M., followed by another short free period. During this time I play cards with my friends, usually cribbage or skat, and win or lose up to a quarter. I hate losing as I usually have a dollar or less of free change, and I think losing shows weak intelligence. My classmate, Rodney, an average student, always wins at cards. I can't figure out why. Playing a good game of cards requires a special form of intelligence, I decide. From 7:30 until 9 there is another study hall. Then we go to bed.

Many nights we have an early, shortened study hall because there is a college event. We get to see all the college athletic contests, plays, concerts; even an opera put on once a year, sung in English. Women from neighboring St. Benedict's College sing the female roles. When I see Strauss's playful *Die Fledermaus* I love the production and develop a taste for opera that lasts all my life. We get to hear outside speakers the college brings to campus. I remember a Negro preacher from Chicago who spoke once. I like to think it was Dr. Martin Luther King, before he was famous. Every Saturday night we can watch a movie. I go to them all. Since I am young I can't find the words to say it, but I know I am receiving a splendid education, with college embellishments. I am free to experience it all. This place has everything.

Except for girls and beer. For that we go to town.

Alcohol

THERE WERE LOTS OF PROHIBITIONS in our central Minnesota, German Catholic culture, but drinking alcohol wasn't one of them. My mother, who was born farther west and raised in the Congregational Church, insisted on citing the law: no drinking until the age of twenty-one, but I thought that was an impossible rule to keep, and I didn't know anyone who waited that long. Dad almost always supported Mother's opinions, but in this case his support was qualified. "It should be OK for the children to have alcohol on special occasions," he said, "in the home. I think the law allows it."

Mother was rigid. "The law says twenty-one."

Dad advanced his case. "Children should learn how to drink at home. In Europe people drink as a family."

So once, at Sunday dinner, he gave us each a small glass of wine. Mother didn't feel she could override his finesse of the law and said nothing. It was port wine, sweet and tart at the same time. I didn't like it. I was fourteen.

Mother noticed my grimace. "So, you don't like it," she said. "Then there's no need to drink it." She seemed pleased. "You can wait until you're twenty-one."

But Mother's opinion was overwhelmed by the attitude

of the community. Aside from her, no one else appeared very much concerned about underage drinking, although the main bars and restaurants in town checked for identification because it was the law.

In high school our religious instructor, Father Fabian, made a distinction between God's law and civil law. We were told to respect civil law, of course—like paying our taxes, which was for the good of society—but I received the impression that certain civil laws, like the one against jaywalking, were of no moral consequence. So I figured the law against underage drinking was like jaywalking. Father told us that alcohol, in itself, was good; that it often enhanced a social occasion and that there was nothing morally wrong with using it. He even seemed to tolerate an occasional unplanned intoxication, sort of like overeating. I received the impression that such behavior would be a mistake, but not morally grievous, a defining term at the time. *Intentional* drunkenness was wrong, of course.

I listened closely to these subtleties and planned my behavior, mentally pushing open the drinking loophole like a prisoner finding an unlocked door. Mother's arguments were legally correct, but they carried no moral weight. I was as free to decide whether to drink as I was to decide what shirt to put on. And I put great weight on the word *intention*. I would drink freely, with good intention. If I went too far, it was accidental. I was free to enjoy the pleasures of drinking, I told myself. High school seemed like a good time to start. Many of my friends had a similar eagerness.

In certain places around our hometown, and especially in the neighboring German Catholic small towns, beer was served pretty much to anyone who looked to be a teenager or older. Teenagers, then, were of working age on the nearby farms and so, by small-town logic, were considered of drinking age also. Most families in and around those towns stopped in the tavern for a drink and conversation every Sunday after Mass. If someone wore a baseball uniform they were served beer without question, since drinking beer after the Sunday game was expected of all players.

I was a sophomore in high school when four of us left the boarding school grounds on a Saturday afternoon in March and hitchhiked four miles to the little town of Avon for some drinking adventure. John "Friday" Luce had the heaviest beard, the strongest voice, and, perhaps most important, an easy nonchalance. He agreed to be our representative and go into a small store to buy a six-pack while the rest of us waited outside. We wondered about our chances, but then were pleased when Friday emerged from the store with a bulky, square-looking package. "I also got cigarettes," he said, so we looked forward to an especially good time.

On the edge of town stood a small, three-sided, makeshift shed with a flat roof, obviously intended to shelter animals. It looked to us like a good place to be out of sight from any judgmental adults. To get there, we had to slip between a barbwire fence and then step carefully through a bumpy marsh. A stiff north wind was blowing, and it was cloudy and cold. The shed looked like good protection. "Let's go there," Friday said, and spread the barbwire so the rest of us could crawl through.

"We're lucky," I said as we entered the shed. "The manure on the floor is crusty."

"No shit," said Friday.

We were able to find a spot of mostly clean ground to stand and then each began to open a can of beer and light a cigarette—four of us, standing there in the cold, dark shed, afraid to touch anything or shift our feet without looking down. I didn't like the taste of beer, nor did I like cigarettes very much, but I said nothing. I was becoming a man. I would learn to like cigarettes and beer. Only sissies didn't like them.

"Here, someone take this," Friday said when he got tired of holding the bag of extra beer. There was no place to set anything, nor anything like a bench to sit on. Sweeney took the bag.

"My hands are cold. Give me another cigarette," I said. Although we were smoking, it did nothing to raise the temperature in the shed. Wind pushed through the cracks and carried the heat away. But soon the beer lifted our spirits, and we began to have a good time.

"Bones, you're starting to get drunk," I said. "You're leaning sideways." Bones was a tall, gangly kid.

"No, I'm not. *You're* drunk," he said.

"I'm standing straight as a two-by-four."

"Yah, from your old man's lumberyard. Warped and full of knotholes," Bones said. I grinned and took a drag from my cigarette. It was hard to inhale deeply. I didn't have the lungs for it. I took another drag and tried to blow smoke rings. The wind scattered them quickly.

"Did you hear about the latest swimming suit for women?" Sweeney asked.

"No."

Sweeney blushed red as sunset. "Two Band Aids and a cork," and he smiled in crinkly-eyed glee. The rest of us giggled nervously.

"Sweeney, you tell the rottenest jokes," I said, "how can there be a priest and a nun in your family?"

"I don't tell *them* the jokes; they're too holy. I learn 'em from my uncle. He's not such a serious Catholic." We opened the extra cans and passed them around.

"Look," I said, "beer's running out of Sweeney's nose."

"No, it's not," Sweeney insisted.

"You're right. It's snot," I said. "It's too damn cold out here."

In an hour or so we finished. "Like the chicken farmer says, 'Let's get the *flock* out of here,'" Friday said.

We hitchhiked back to school and tried to look normal.

A group of classmates was standing in the main hall as we entered. "Hall, what are you doing with that shit-eating grin on your face?" one of them inquired.

"Nothing," I said, "but you guys sure missed a good time."

"No, we didn't. We went to St. Joe and had some beer. Fredrichs just threw up in the wastebasket. We had a great time, too."

As I moved into higher grades I concentrated on learning how to hold my beer. That is, I would drink to see how much I could hold. Sometimes I miscalculated and had to make a quick trip outside, but in the process, I felt, I was learning to become a man. "He's the kind of guy who can hold his beer," I'd hear adults say, always with admiration. I wanted to be that kind of guy and still have that carefree feeling, that easy good nature that came from drinking beer, lots of it. Some of my classmates had the same need.

"Wolkerstorfer and I went to town today. I had twelve beers," said Mahowald one day.

"I had fourteen," said Wolkerstorfer.

I knew they were lying. Nobody could hold twelve beers without reeling to the floor, and for sure not fourteen. But maybe they were one-upping the rest of us at our foolish game. Maybe it was a parody of us. All I could say was, "I don't believe you. Fourteen is an awful lot of beer."

Driving, of course, was a problem for anyone who drank too much, but there were far fewer cars on the road then, so the chances of an accident were much reduced. But there were accidents, sometimes deadly ones. My father constantly warned me not to drink and drive. But people in general seemed to look upon the accidents as one of those unfortunate things that can't be changed, sort of like injuries in an NFL game now, or death in a war. "That's the way it is," they said. As far as I know, no one thought seriously of changing the rules, until the Mothers Against Drunk Driving came along later and saved us all from ourselves.

We had our own little driving episodes. Once, after a Sunday game of baseball against St. Wendel, another nearby small town, followed by an hour or two of drinking beer, we teammates were driving home on a gravel road in Butch Fish's old roadster, laughing at nothing as people in high spirits do. The road took a sharp turn left. Butch cranked the steering wheel too late. We skidded off the gravel and into the ditch, jolted but unhurt. We sat for a minute, laughing, then the rest of us got out of the car and lifted and pushed, while Butch worked the gas. Within minutes we had the car back on the road, laughed again, and drove away. Running off the road happened quite often in those days, even when the driver was sober, especially during winter because of the ice and snow, but almost every time we were able to push the car back onto solid footing.

In college I wanted to go to hard liquor places such as the El Paso and the Press Bar rather than small-town beer joints, but to do so I needed an identification card. The people who checked IDs seemed not to care much whether they were official. They seemed to care only that we had one—men, that is; they never checked women. I learned from another student that I could easily fix my college identification card by taking an ink pen and extending two lines up from the 7 on my birth date so that it looked like a 4 and then magically I was three years older. I assumed it was the checkers' responsibility to find out whether I was fraudulent. They never seemed to care. After all, the business's preference was to serve customers, not turn them away at the door. I worried about the sinfulness of my little lie, however. Would I have to tell the priest in confession and promise to try to change my ways when I knew it would not be sincere? I had created a lie, all right, and it was intentional, but was it serious? I decided it was a small transgression versus the opportunity it provided—going to nice places, relaxing with liquor, and meeting girls—and I decided God would just have to accept the choices a young

man sometimes made. I would burn it off in purgatory. I did
not confess it.

After four years at St. John's Prep and two years at the college, I considered myself well versed in the liberal arts and
thought it would be good to transfer to another school and
specialize in some sort of profession. I enrolled at Marquette
University in the city of Milwaukee, noting carefully that it
was Catholic also. But there were other forces at work. My
high school friend, Rodney, had been writing me letters telling me about fraternity life, about beautiful, dark-haired girls
with Irish and Italian names, and about the flowing beer. I
wanted an education, of course, but I wanted all the rest,
too. It seemed like a cornucopia. I enrolled in the university's School of Business. And when I got there, I was not
disappointed.

Milwaukee was a town of significant population, but char-
acterized by industry more than culture, and was overshadowed
by Chicago, its big neighbor to the south. It was a city of
numerous breweries and a preponderance of German and
Polish factory workers who enjoyed their drink. There were
taverns everywhere, to me as interesting as each of the individual farms in central Minnesota. I wanted to experience
them all. Because many factories worked evening shifts, the
bars remained open until 2 A.M. on weekdays and 3:30 A.M.
on weekends. Many would reopen again at 6 A.M. to serve the
workers coming off overnight shifts.

I learned of the city's official attitude toward alcohol when
I was responsible for organizing a party for the residents on

our college dormitory floor. We planned to hold it in an outdoor park, so I called the city to ask about the rules.

"Is there an ordinance against having a keg of beer in a city park?"

"Yes, there is."

"Is it enforced?"

"No, it is not."

"Thank you. Good-bye."

The priests had taught that in order for a law to have meaning it had to be enforced. So the city's answer sounded wonderful. I was in drinking paradise. After six years on a campus in the woods of central Minnesota and only occasional forays into town, I felt I had moved from the outer fringes of the village carnival right into the midway. And I enjoyed it. When I visited the workingman's bars, I learned to drink a shot of whiskey with a beer chaser, a real quick way to alcohol bliss. Otherwise, I simply drank beer with my fellow students.

But I got into trouble drinking in Milwaukee. Once, after a party, I was driving my date's car and accidentally drove into the car ahead of me that was stopped for a traffic light, behavior that is difficult to excuse or explain away. The attending police officer pulled me aside to an empty parking lot.

"Stand on one leg," he said. I stretched my arms and did as told, wobbling a little, but succeeding for the most part, I thought.

"Now walk down this line," he demanded and pointed to a yellow parking line on the pavement. "Put one foot directly in front of the other." I did as he said, wobbling a little, but again feeling like I probably passed for sober.

"Open your eyes." He shined his flashlight directly into my pupils.

"Follow my finger," he said, as he moved it close to my nose. I thought I must have passed that test too, but he was not done yet.

He threw a handful of coins on the ground and told me to pick them up. I concentrated very hard. Then I picked them up, very carefully, and handed them to him. I thought I performed quite well.

"Name them," he said.

Name them? I was blank. I had no recollection at all. I had concentrated so hard on picking them up without wavering that I simply had not noticed what they were, nor how many there were. So I guessed at the answers, and figured he had me. A sober person would know the answers easily, I imagined. Well, it turned out I was lucky. He simply gave me a warning and let me go.

On another occasion my friend Frank and I were coming from a party in downtown Milwaukee. It was time to go home, but I wanted to continue the fun. "Let's go to a hotel," I suggested, "and ask if they have any women." If the answer was yes, I didn't know what we would do; we weren't thinking that far ahead. Just asking seemed adventurous enough. But if we were introduced to some women, they would know we could enjoy a drink together since I had a whiskey bottle sticking out of the pocket of my sport coat. We would talk, I imagined, and tease about possibilities but do nothing about them. On the other hand, if something happened, I didn't intend it, of course. I could tell the priest in confession it had just happened. So I composed myself, leaned on the counter, and asked the hotel clerk politely, "Sir, do you have any women here?" It was innocent enough, I thought. We didn't ask to do anything bad. It was just a query. Maybe he would think we were some kind of inspectors. Who knows? It was the start of a conversation.

The clerk went in the back room. It was getting exciting. Maybe he would send some sexy women out. We could have a nice talk, I thought, a titillating talk. Frank and I sat down to wait.

Moments later two policemen grabbed us, took us outside, threw us in a paddy wagon, and drove off. I was incensed. What did we do to be treated so rudely? We were college students just enjoying ourselves. I realized, slowly, that the hotel clerk had not played our game.

I was placed in a cell by myself. I hollered periodically that I had a right to make a phone call, something I had learned from listening to older people talk about their rights when apprehended by police. My pleas were ignored. I hollered again. Still no one listened. In the morning an officer came in and asked who was insisting on making a phone call. Bewildered now, I told him it was me.

"The phone's right over there," he said.

"You bet. Thank you. I'll make a call." After such a fuss, I had to follow through.

But who would I call? I wondered, now a little more sober. Surely not my parents, nor the school authorities. Not a lawyer—I didn't know any. So I faked a call to somebody back at the dormitory, then returned to my cell in confident stride, but without meeting the officer's eyes so that he couldn't see how foolish I felt.

Frank and I spent the rest of the morning in the drunk tank—I believe it was called —along with about twenty other scofflaws arrested during the night. They looked awful. Some had been in fights. Some were chronic drunks. Their disheveled clothes smelled. We, at least, were wearing sport coats. Some mumbled or spoke nonsense. We, on the other hand, spoke to each other in full sentences, wondering what the hell would happen next.

About noon we were brought before a judge. We said nothing. A policeman explained to the judge that we were college students who got carried away drinking, but that we had no previous offenses. Without additional comment, the judge dismissed our case. We looked at each other in stunned relief.

Once away from the jail, Frank started to laugh. I laughed, too, first a little, and then some more, and then I couldn't control it. It shook every cell in my body. Frank also exploded in laughter. It felt wonderful, this laughing. We were on the street and I thought I should compose myself, but every time I looked at him, I couldn't. He just kept rippling with laughter and then so did I. Finally, he caught his breath and tried to bring up a line from the night before.

"Do . . ." giggle. "Do . . ." giggle. "Do you have any girls?" Then a roar of laughter. I couldn't help it either. I held my sides and doubled up, almost falling to the ground.

"*Sir*, do you have any girls?" I added, and seized my stomach to keep from falling apart.

"That mumbling drunk was nuts, absolutely nuts," Frank said, and laughed amid gasps for air. "He kept talking to me. I was worried he wanted to be my friend." This brought on a new round of tumult.

"Why not?" I mocked. "You had a lot in common."

"Yes," he laughed through squinting eyes.

"And I forgot my whiskey." I said, and guffawed so loudly it rattled the buildings. "Do you think we should go back?"

Finally, Frank settled down enough to deliver a straight sentence. "We made a trip to hell and returned safely." Then we laughed again and kept on laughing until tears ran.

Before I had left the courtroom, however, I couldn't help overhearing the next case, one involving a young black man who was in some trouble that sounded no worse than ours, and he was fined ten dollars. I felt uneasy. It looked to me as if we benefited from being white and in college. I held my peace, of course, and was grateful for my good fortune, but I noticed the difference.

Over time, I matured and began to drink more carefully. Public attitudes changed also. Getting drunk is no longer an excusable mistake or an amusement. It is an irresponsible stupidity.

Hot Ass

SOMETIMES THE PREFECTS running our boarding school got physical with a wayward student: a cuff on the ear, a squeeze on the arm so tight it stopped circulation, a knuckle rap on the back of the head. And why not? They were dealing with teenage boys who needed taming.

American society held no censure for rough discipline. The movies were full of women slapping somebody or cowboys punching each other straight in the teeth. In our schools and homes we were given to believe that the idea of discipline itself was very important not the method of delivery. An undisciplined boy was heading for a life of trouble, we learned. Better to bend his will to good habits at a young age; he will see it as a favor later. Voluntary compliance was best; but if it was not forthcoming, then physical coercion was acceptable. And in prep school we were in a male environment. Men understood physical discipline.

But our boarding school had a special variation on this matter of discipline. If a senior caught an underclassman violating a rule—such as going to town without permission or smoking cigarettes—he would report the violation to his class. His word was accepted without question, and the miscreant would be in line for discipline. Also, we had heard that the prefect, on occasion, might suggest to a few leaders of the senior class that they "shape up" a troublesome boy. Everyone understood what this meant. The unfortunate one would be taken to a handball court in the basement of the gymnasium, ordered to lower his pants, and given a whipping. Each senior was entitled to deliver two swats with his belt. The process was called, informally, a "hot ass."

A few hot asses were administered in my freshman year— discreet affairs. I'm not sure who got them, and since I wasn't affected personally I didn't pay much attention.

But in my sophomore year they became frequent. The seniors somehow seemed to be especially good at finding underclassmen involved in various infractions. One day my brother Bob, a freshman, and his buddy, Pinky Shuck, a Negro from St. Paul, got caught smoking. A hot ass was scheduled immediately for that evening after supper. I was fearful for Bob— Pinky too, he was a little guy—but mostly for Bob, since our blood ran together. Bob was strong, but he didn't like pain. He could wail when he got hurt. The senior class had gained a reputation for enjoying hot asses. They were becoming increasingly violent.

There was no possibility to appeal the decision. Smoking by freshmen was forbidden. It would do no good to tell our parents, who believed in discipline; or the school authorities, who tacitly endorsed the activity. The punishment for Bob seemed unavoidable.

That night, I arrived at the handball court hoping to witness Bob and Pinky's scheduled hot ass. But I was ushered away. I was not to see what would happen, a senior told me.

So I left the building and stood outside, listening by the windows, which were opaque.

I was alone in the darkness. It would be nice to have a cigarette, I thought, to settle my nerves, but quickly dismissed the thought. Sophomores were not allowed to smoke either. Then I heard a cry of fear and pain. I thought it was Bob, but I wasn't sure. Which was it? Fear? Or pain? As a little boy, Bob sometimes hollered in anticipation of a spanking. I thought he did it to gain sympathy, to lighten the strokes. But, once, when we both had a spanking coming, he put little wooden slats in his pants and still wailed with conviction even before Dad whacked him with the yardstick. I was puzzled by that convincing behavior. Then through the window came another cry of hurt. I thought it was Bob and felt afraid for him. Even if it were Pinky screaming, I thought, Bob would be next and it would be the same. Whoever it was, the screams didn't sound fake. They were howls of anguish. I waited by the window, helpless, wincing with each outburst. I was quite sure it was pain. Still more cries came. I could only stare into the darkness and try to count the numbers, hoping for the end. Perhaps twenty-five seniors participated, two blows each, times two victims. One hundred blows. I counted, but I didn't hear them all. Eventually the squeals of pain became irregular. Perhaps some seniors swung easy; I could only guess. Then, finally there was silence. Empathy for Bob drained from my body, and my own buttocks relaxed. I trusted it was over.

A couple of concerned students and I joined Bob and Pinky in the gym locker room. I checked Bob's backside. There was redness from the blows, but no bleeding. Pinky would not let us check him. He didn't like us rubbing his nappy hair on other occasions, and he didn't want us inspecting his backside now either. But Pinky looked chastened. He'd had a shocking experience. And so had Bob.

The seniors kept up the discipline. When my classmate Tom Gorman, from Chicago, got his third hot ass of the year, he ran away from school. He went out to the highway and simply hitchhiked away. Disappeared, as far as we knew, although we heard he had probably gone to a relative's house somewhere in St. Paul. Gorman was not a bad kid. He just had a hard time living with the rules, or he had a hard time being discreet about his violations, unlike the rest of us. Gorman's was the tenth hot ass that year, and there were still a few months left in the school year.

The prefects, along with the headmaster, must have decided that the disciplinary occasions were getting too frequent, and with Gorman running away they were not having the desired effect. As authorities, they could have simply outlawed the behavior, but they thought it was a discussable subject and that it should involve all students, so they scheduled a convocation in the campus auditorium. The term *hot ass*, of course, was never mentioned. It was called a discussion about discipline.

The convocation began with a panel of student academic leaders giving comments and opinions. One considered "the positive and negative implications of such corrective behavior." Another said he "deplored the untoward discipline, but thought that perhaps it was necessary." All agreed that discipline was important. After half an hour of such fatuous blather the audience was invited to comment and ask questions. More polite observations ensued, along with a couple of short speeches.

Finally, junior Chick Hayden could stand it no longer. He rose from his seat and fairly shouted his convictions.

"Let's call them what they are: hot asses. And let's admit they are violent." He paused to collect his thoughts. "We've got kids running away from school. Let's get rid of these hot asses. I say, outlaw them." The audience erupted in applause. He had released everyone's unspoken thoughts in a moment of stark truth. Additional comments suddenly were no longer relevant. The attitude of the student body was evident. The headmaster and prefects apparently felt the same, and the meeting was adjourned. The next day the headmaster issued a ruling outlawing discipline of that type.

Democracy worked. It was early spring of 1953. Perhaps we were part of a larger movement, for much of society would change its attitude about physical punishment in the years that followed. Bob and Pinky recovered. We never heard from Gorman again. In our school there would no longer be flushed, swollen behinds.

A couple of generations have passed. Discipline is not nearly so strict. In fact, many would say that it's nonexistent; that, instead, children's desires are indulged. It's a good thing physical punishment has mostly been banished, but we as a society seem to be struggling with how to replace it, or whether we should. Youngsters today have a culture that gives them great freedom. They would giggle at the term *hot ass*, I imagine, and assume it means something sexy.

The Surprise Season

NOBODY EXPECTED MUCH of our football teams during my early years at prep school. We had not won a conference game in two years, and we were arrayed against powerful opponents—Minneapolis DeLaSalle, St. Thomas and Cretin from St. Paul, and St. Cloud Cathedral—in a five-team conference. Four large urban schools and us, a little boarding school in the central Minnesota woods with half the student body studying for the priesthood. But we had hopes for ourselves; we knew we could improve over previous years, as long as no leading player got injured.

Quarterback was a vital position. The quarterback called the plays, but more important, he handled the ball on almost every play. A year earlier, Coach Ebnet had changed from the old single-wing formation in which the ball was centered directly to a running back, to the then new T-formation. Under the old alignment the quarterback was mainly a blocker. Under the new, he received the ball and initiated the play. He was the universal joint in the football machine. To carry out those responsibilities Ebnet chose Phil Hammer, a 5 foot 6 inch, 130-pound, frail, sandy-haired priesthood student. Until then, Hammer had been an acceptable but not exceptional halfback. He could outrun many, but not everybody, and he could throw a forward pass probably twenty yards at the most. Fullback Joe Mahowald would be asked to throw longer balls. But Hammer was smart, cool, and reliable. Those characteristics were very important.

In the first game, against nonconference opponent Little Falls, Hammer called a nicely balanced mix of plays, and our Preps led 6–0 at halftime. Early in the second half he called a play in which he carried the ball. He ran left behind his line, faked a pitchout, then cut upfield, turned on his speed and raced, untouched, eighty yards for a touchdown. He looked like the fastest man on the field on that particular play. We went on to win the game 12–0. It looked like we had a new offensive threat, little Phil Hammer, to go with our larger, stronger, regular running backs. Our offense might be difficult to stop.

But Coach Ebnet was alarmed. In front of the whole team he told Hammer not to call a play in which he carried the ball. He was simply too valuable, Coach said; we could not afford to get him injured. A solid hit from a 200 pounder might knock him out for the season, might cause his little frame to split in half. Without him we would be a team struggling for leadership. "We have stronger backs, just as quick, who can carry the ball," Coach said. "Hammer, you're our brains, our playmaker." Hammer was a priesthood student; he obeyed orders. He accepted his role.

We then beat nearby rival, St. Cloud Cathedral 20–2. Senior halfback Joe Machtemes scored two touchdowns. Machtemes was fast, a low-hurdler on the track team, and he hit the line in a low driving style, as though leaning over hurdles. Once beyond the line of scrimmage, he liked to cut back against the flow, weave and pick up extra blockers, then surprise the defense with his speed. He carried himself confidently and because of his black stubble beard looked more mature than anybody on the team. He emerged as the principal ball carrier, the guy who would carry when we needed the yards. But we had to worry about Machtemes; he was vulnerable, too. A year earlier he had broken his wrist in the third game of the season. Like a warrior, he finished that game in spite of his wrist, but he was done for the season. This year, when he carried the ball, we watched in admiration but we also crossed our fingers. He was our best ball player.

A week later we played Cretin in St. Paul. Machtemes scored two touchdowns, one sixty-seven yards long. Right halfback Gerry Hassett scored two also, including one for forty-nine yards. Hassett was a transfer student and proved to be a big factor in our improvement from the ineffectual season the year before. A heavy-bellied 220 pounder, he was slow at the start but accelerated like a buffalo in open field. He complemented the shiftier Machtemes beautifully. The final score against Cretin: 25–0.

Next, we beat Marshall 16–0 in a nonconference game, with Machtemes and Hassett each scoring touchdowns.

The following week, we met St. Thomas for their homecoming. Machtemes scored twice and backup halfback, speedster Ron Neidzielski scored from twenty-five yards out in the last seconds of the game. St. Thomas was held scoreless. We were the victors, 20–0. Five games had passed, three against tough conference teams, and no one had scored a touchdown against our boys from the woods.

A showdown was looming. Mighty DeLaSalle, led by coach Dick Reinhardt, had been undefeated the previous season and was on its way to a perfect record this season as well. They ran precision power plays with lots of blockers and blasted out victories. Defeating them would require heroic effort.

The Preps were playing at home in nature's bowl surrounded by the red, orange, and yellow leaves of autumn. Beautiful it was, brightened with sun, but all attention went to the game. At midfield, the sod, scuffed to stubble and dirt from previous battles, suggested a looming collision, a test for dominance.

DeLaSalle grabbed the lead early with a seventy-one-yard touchdown run, and followed with an extra point. It was an ominous start. But our Preps followed up with a drive the full length of the field, and retaliated on a two-yard plunge by little Phil Hammer. Coach Ebnet held his breath; he also held his tongue. Hammer was not insubordinate; he was simply calling the unexpected, gutsy play. Our boys missed a run at the extra point; we didn't have a reliable kicker. DeLaSalle led 7–6. The teams then traded yardage and punts in a standoff for the rest of the first half.

At halftime, Coach Ebnet was his usual restrained, analytical self. He let the team settle down for a few minutes, then gave out helpful observations and suggestions.

"McNeil, play a little deeper on passing situations. Dold, drift outside on those sweeps. Kennedy, you too. Let the defensive end hold the inside." He paused to let it sink in.

Then he turned to Hammer. "Keep calling those plays up the middle. We seem to be able to move the ball there with ease. Our boys are handling their front line well. Keep working on that middle. Give the ball to Machtemes, or Hassett on a counterplay."

Then he closed with a confidence-building, low-key exhortation to the whole team. "We've played 'em basically even, boys. We're able to control the line. This second half will make the season. It's a special opportunity. LET'S GO DO IT!" Then he led the team in a prayer to the Blessed Virgin. We returned to the field, resolute.

Our team received the second-half kickoff. Down the field we pushed as the front line created repeated openings—we were the precision machine now, not the boys from Minneapolis—and finally we scored, as Machtemes plunged straight ahead on short yardage right into the end zone. The stadium erupted in wild ovation. Our team was proving its competitive strength. We were leading 12–7. But once more they stopped us on the extra points.

Machtemes, what a beautiful name right then. Three syllables, with the accent on the first. He was carrying us to victory. Could be the name of a German war machine, or a space rocket at warp speed. Fits rhythmically with Bademus, Fidelis, and Paternus—ancient saints. That's it, a new football chant:

> *Machtemes, Bademes, Fidelis, and Paternus.*
> *Nobody can match our boys blest, nor burn us.*

He would be raised to sainthood this day, that Machtemes, by us anyway, because he was sent by God to give us victory over Goliath from Minneapolis. With his teammates Drotzman,

George and Bernard Ostertag, Pasch, Hayes, Andresen, Montreuil, and all the rest, they would be our new litany of saints. Those of us on the bench held our breath and *believed*.

In the fourth quarter DeLaSalle scored on another grinding assault and took the lead 13–12. God had forsaken us. Both teams were Catholic, but we were surely more deserving. The game was moving away from our grasp. We were not able to stop them like we had other teams. Maybe they were better. Maybe this was as far as we would go. But there was time yet for another effort.

Then God chose. Or was it us? We drove the field and He sent Saint Machtemes into the end zone from fifteen yards out. We exploded in joy. The game was ours if we could end it now. But there were still four minutes left. We took our seats again and strained under the enduring tension.

Mahowald kicked off to their twenty. The receiver tried to go left, then cut back right but there was no opening. Scheuren and George Ostertag each got a shoulder into him and brought him down. The clock ticked on. They got a first down. Then another. They kept running plays but made no progress. Then time ran out. Our boys had held. We realized we had won the championship game 19–13. Now the jubilation was unrestrained. It was glorious. We carried Coach Ebnet off the field.

In the final game of the season we beat previously unbeaten Melrose on their field 14–7. Machtemes was injured. Hassett, although slowed by an ankle sprain, scored two touchdowns.

A week later Coach Ebnet summed up the season at a special banquet. The team scored 126 points to the opponents' 22. We

COACH CHUB EBNET'S CHAMPION PREPS. *First Row:* Hall,
J. Mahowald, Pasch, Co-captains Ostertag and Machtemes, Kennedy,
Schreiner. *Second Row:* Drotzman, Hayes, Hassett, Hammer, Andresen,
Montreuil, Folsom. *Third Row:* Coach Ebnet, Scheuren, B. Ostertag, Mowry,
Friederichs, Fairbanks, McNeil, Spano, Parnell, Trainer Corcoran, Hall.
Fourth Row: Honer, Dold, Moch, Ehli, Holmes, R. Mahowald, De La Cruz,
Niedzielski.

The champions, autumn 1953.

won the Central Catholic Conference. We were undefeated.
Joe Machtemes was selected Catholic All-State. But the quiet
leader on the team, Coach Ebnet said, was . . . right tackle,
George Ostertag. Hardworking, dependable George, a blond
Aryan, 5 feet 10, 170 pounds, chest shaped like a heart; quick,
never off balance, the lead blocker on all plays to his side of
the line; a farm boy with an easy smile; his work spoke for
him. On defense he was the middle linebacker, the mind
and soul of a unit that held four teams scoreless, one to two
points, and the remaining two to a combined total of three

touchdowns. He should have received all-state honors, along with Machtemes, but there seemed to be an understanding that only one player from each team would be chosen and Machtemes had the scoring title. George, instead, earned the high esteem of his coach and teammates.

All the players made a contribution, of course. The brilliance of Coach Ebnet was to fill out the minor roles on the team with ordinary but tough athletes and make them specialists at various positions. Some played offense, some defense, a few both ways. The undefeated season proved his special ability. But without Hammer, the steady quarterback; Machtemes, the star halfback; Hassett, the alternative threat; and quiet George Ostertag, the team would have been quite ordinary. With them it was outstanding.

That wasn't all. We were part of the St. John's community; and the university football team, the older brothers in our campus family, tied for the championship in their league that season—their first title in fifteen years. They were overachievers also. Two of the starters were freshmen linemen Chuck Froehle and Harry LaRose, both graduates of our hapless Prep team of the previous year. Froehle played with boundless enthusiasm and grit—guard on offense, linebacker on defense—and received all-conference recognition. LaRose, an Ojibway from northern Minnesota, had great ability at center and played well but suffered from injuries. We were proud of our brothers. We were proud of their championship also.

The leader of that successful university season was a twenty-six-year-old, first-year coach, John Gagliardi. He was a modest, good-natured fellow. We didn't know then he would stay for fifty years and become a national celebrity for his record of victories, but we knew he could coach.

Who knows where success lies? Who knows tomorrow's fortune? Who knows when to carry the ball in spite of orders? Who knows the role of God versus personal effort? Who knows what star coach is disguised in gentle humor? None of us. We toil every day and hope for the best. Occasionally we act against orders and trust in God. We learn to treat the average man as a future star because in some way he may be. We learn that winning is important and we try hard. But God may fool us. We may not win the games we want. We may dwell among losers in life. We may stumble in rudeness and greed. But the monks taught us we would find happiness if we pursued it and our hearts were pure. They couldn't tell us we would be successful on the field of play. But they could and did tell us to accept the joy humbly when it came. It does come. We learned *that* in the fall of 1953 in the strange game of rushing a football to the end zone.

Sweat

WE CHILDREN CALLED IT SWEAT; Mother called it perspiration. Mother liked to choose special words. She used
verbs like *crex* and *gallivant* and *dawdle*, and she didn't tolerate
crudeness. She would correct me when I said "hind end." I
had assumed it was an improvement over *ass*, which of course
was not allowed. "Seat," she said. "The word is *seat*." Dad was
not so fussy; but he did smack my brother Bob awfully hard
once when he called me a "cocksucker." Bob was very young,
and I felt sorry for him because I was sure he didn't know
what it meant. I didn't know what it meant and I was older.
We both learned that day that it was not a good word to use
around the house or, by extension, in front of Grandma or
priests or nuns.

Whatever its name, sweat or perspiration was a part of
everyday life. There was no air conditioning in cars or homes.
Everybody had to deal with the body's glandular flow. Mother
hated sweat—er, perspiration. When the weather got hot she
put Kleenex under her arms. On the worst summer days she
would keep the house closed tight and the blinds down to
preserve the overnight coolness. I thought the house was dark
and stuffy that way and wanted to throw open the windows,

let in a breeze, and sweat if I had to, but Mother had control of the house during the daytime hours.

A few theaters and restaurants had air-conditioning. Because it was so unusual they would promote it with prominent signs like "It's Cool Inside," or simply "Air Conditioned." Certainly it improved business on hot days.

Because we sweat in those days doesn't mean we didn't wear proper clothes. A man would wear an undershirt—to absorb the sweat—and then a dress shirt or a work shirt on top. For Sunday church all adult men wore an undershirt, starched white shirt, suit, and tie regardless of the heat. Ballplayers, who sweat and got dirty besides, wore a sweatshirt and then a thick uniform shirt over that. I was a catcher in my young days on the ball diamond and usually had to share a facemask with the opposing catcher. At the end of half an inning he would hand the soggy mask to me. I would return it half an inning later. We learned to ignore the unpleasantness of placing our face in each other's rim of sweat.

Laborers would sweat all day, then stop in a tavern for a cool beer before going home, usually on foot. Working ladies might have a semicircle of perspiration seeping around the armpits of their dresses.

I worked in a laundry at the St. Cloud Hospital one summer, pulling sheets, pillowcases, and other linens from big washers. Two of us would lean into one tumbler and work side by side. I think it was the summer with three straight weeks of over ninety-degree temperature and a few days topping a hundred. I was in high school and experimenting with deodorant. One roll-on that I tried, by midday, turned on me. It smelled like, oh, perhaps Limburger cheese. It made a compost pile seem savory. I felt sorry for the guy working next to me, and tried to pull sheets from the tumbler without extending my arms, which of course didn't work. The next day I tried my older brother's Mennen squirt deodorant and that worked fine. I used that brand with success—I think—for forty-five years. A simple squeeze made it squirt, and it gave off a nice fragrance; it was perfect. But they discontinued it. Had they told me before making their decision, I would have bought enough to last my grandchildren into old age. I liked it that much. With or without deodorant, we still sweat plenty in that laundry. And so did the girls who steam-ironed the sheets and pillowcases in an adjacent space. I could see the semicircles under their arms.

One sultry August night there was a dance at the armory in town. The music was hot. We teenagers danced "swing" wildly until sweat gushed from our faces and saturated our clothes. The armory's low, semicircular roof trapped our accumulated, sticky body heat until everyone was dripping, but the music was so good we didn't care; the atmosphere was deliciously uncomfortable. Near the end of the night, I finished an exuberant dance with an unknown partner, then wiped a hanky over my brow. The music turned slow. I thought we were done, too wet to dance again. But my partner, whoever she was, with rivulets running down her face, raised her arms to continue dancing. I embraced her naturally, and we continued the dance, body to body, cheek to cheek, sweat running together, feet moving to the unrushed beat. Maybe it was perspiration, not sweat. I don't know, but it was wonderful, accepting each other just as we were without apology or pretense, blending our young emotions and the body's natural flow.

Forbidden Sex

SORRY, THERE'S NOTHING of interest here, since sex was indeed forbidden and there was the overriding terror of unintended pregnancy. To borrow a line from a comedian, the sexual revolution started twenty minutes after I got married.

Work

IF THERE WERE ANY SLACKERS in St. Cloud, I didn't know them. Everybody worked. The housewives did wash on Monday, ironing on Tuesday, baking on Wednesday, cleaning on Thursday, and so on for six days of the week. I may be mixing the wrong tasks with the wrong days, because I wasn't paying close attention at the time, but I knew women had a job every day and I hadn't even considered the general activities of fixing the meals, taking care of the kids, mending clothes, darning socks, church work, and special projects like canning, preparing Thanksgiving dinner, buying birthday and Christmas presents, spring housecleaning, and writing letters.

Women who weren't housewives worked as clerks in stores, or as cooks, or as receptionists and bookkeepers (sometimes combined as one job), or nurses or teachers. All of my grade school teachers were women, members of a religious order. Generally they had forty students in a class. They toiled over class preparations at night. If they perspired under this heavy load, I couldn't tell; they were clothed in black habits, but, for sure, they worked hard.

Men's work was divided by education into the professions

or physical labor. The professionals were doctors, lawyers, dentists, and an occasional banker. They wore suits and worked downtown. There were also priests, more priests than bankers. There were no researchers, programmers, counselors, planners, or technicians in our town.

The laborers worked with their brawn. They helped "switch" trains (that is, they arranged cars in proper order), or they loaded and unloaded boxcars. They built, wired, and plumbed houses. They drove trucks. They delivered mail on foot. They quarried and polished granite. They farmed. Some of the old-timers, Dad said, put on a suit of long underwear in the fall and didn't remove it until spring. Generally, these men worked until their bodies gave out, or until their pensions started, if they were lucky enough to have one.

Somewhere in between were the shopkeepers: butchers, grocers, jewelers, druggists, clothing merchants, and hardware store owners. Their jobs were often physical too, but they dealt with the public and dressed a little better than the manual laborers.

My father worked in the family lumberyard, along with three of his brothers, as shopkeepers on a larger scale. Besides lumber, they sold coal and heating oil. My father waited on customers, estimated construction requirements, wrote up orders, and made sure "the help," that is, the laborers, got the deliveries out. Sometimes he was in the yard himself helping load a truck with materials. Like almost everyone at the time he worked six days a week, ten hours a day, with time off for dinner at noon, the main meal.

On Sundays nobody worked. Nobody shopped either; the stores were closed. Everyone I knew went to church and then socialized. Everyone had the day off, except for the women who prepared meals.

I admired my father's work, which seemed like a salesman-manager job, one step above physical labor. Sometimes he wore suit clothes with an open shirt to work. Because of the size of the business, people seemed to think he had a comfortable, moneyed job. He didn't acknowledge this apparent status, however. He made clear to me that the work he really respected was physical labor. He may not have done it intentionally; but it came through in the conversations I heard.

"Farm kids know how to work," he would say, as did almost everyone in our community, and in a tone that seemed to say: city kids didn't. The attitude was so universally accepted, the term *farmwork* almost seemed to define work. My father expanded the definition, though, as he told of laborers and their activities at the lumberyard.

He admired George Mangel. George would deliver heating oil at midnight on Christmas in below-zero weather if necessary. George was loyal, dependable. He didn't side with those malcontents who wanted to form a union. "George treats his truck like furniture," Father said one evening at supper. "Many of the others are careless."

He talked about Hess, who took care of the horses and lived in the house next to the barn. In earlier times Hess made sure the horses were fed and harnessed and ready to go as soon as the workers arrived to start their deliveries. "He gives more than a day's work for a day's pay," Father said. There was no mention of overtime.

Father idolized Matt Rader and his enthusiasm for work.

Matt treated every job as a contest, to see how much he could do and how fast. A coal company held a competition near the ore docks in Duluth one year, so the lumberyard decided to enter Matt. Most of the contestants were big, hardened Slavs and Scandinavians used to working with ore and coal on the trains going to and from the iron mines. Matt was small and wiry. The others smiled at him skeptically. That day Matt was quickest to empty twenty tons of coal, half a boxcar, and won first prize, $100. Matt competed to be best in every job he did at the lumberyard. "He'd make the horses run when he made deliveries," Dad said.

My older brother Richard came home with stories, too. "We unloaded bricks today. Pretty soon we were comparing to see who could lift the most, just squeezing them together. Big Ed picked up twenty of them."

"A young man has to learn to work," Father would say, and I took it as a personal admonition.

What did he mean, learn to work? Wasn't I smart enough? I could see how to lift and pile and load, and surely I could do as I saw. I was a teenager, though, and hadn't tried it.

At various times during my high school summers Dad assigned me simple jobs around the lumberyard, hoeing weeds between the lumber piles or painting the coal sheds. I found the work tedious and uninteresting. When I got tired, I rested. I knew such behavior didn't meet my father's standards, even though he didn't comment on it. "You're getting a chance to learn how to work," he said.

The summer I worked in a hospital laundry, pulling sheets and towels out of washing machines, my arms ached. I would sit down and rest. I knew an adult worker wouldn't indulge in that comfort, but I did it anyway. I had gotten tired. For two summers I was a carpenter's apprentice, a job I got through my father. The carpenter-teacher told me one day that his twelve-year-old son was handier than I. He was right. I was left-handed and awkward at the work. In my early college years I spent two summers as a counselor at a camp, teaching canoeing and swimming and looking after boys. Some might call that work, but it didn't fit the impressions my father had given me about work; it was too easy. I enjoyed being a counselor but had the uneasy feeling I might never get the chance to do real work as I would soon graduate and my summer opportunities would be over.

In the summer before my senior year in college, I got to work "on construction." Everyone knew that this meant highway construction. Guys who worked on construction developed muscles and suntans, and they made good wages. I was eager to work on construction. I would truly learn how to work and I would develop a Charles Atlas body. The job was right on the edge of downtown St. Cloud, part of a highway underpass project. We were to work in a hole about twenty feet deep. Steel pilings held back the earth. The hole had to be dug deeper but the pilings could not be driven down because they hit "hard pan" as the foreman called it: sand and gravel packed like concrete. Groundwater seeped into the hole. Three or four of us had the job of digging beneath those pilings to loosen the soil with either a shovel or a jackhammer. We were given wading boots. Since the water was up to our ankles, we could not see what we were digging.

Every morning we walked a plank from the ground up to

the top of the pilings and then descended inside the hole by ladder, a shaky and dangerous descent. It is hard to be nimble in wading boots. The hole was maybe fifteen feet square, too narrow to get a full range of sun. We spent eight hours a day working on the hard pan down in the earth, standing in water, with constant jackhammer noise. This, I decided, was my opportunity to learn to work as Father had described it. I chose to attack the work like Matt Rader, to be first down the ladder, to never rest, and to work until quitting time even if we only loosened two inches that day, and then to show up the next morning before starting time. When the foremen said he needed another worker, I suggested my brother Bob. The foreman said, "OK, tell him to come by in the morning," and he hired him.

I tried to set an example for my brother. When the jackhammer made my shoulders tired, I kept on working. When scratching with the shovel yielded nothing but sand and a few stones, I kept on scratching. I cleared the way for other guys when they were working. I never rested. When the foreman said we could break, I worked a little longer as though there were one more rock I had to get free. I was proving to myself that I could do this work. I was trying to impress my fellow workers, my foreman, and myself. I did this day after day, asking nothing but regular pay in return. Dad had said, "A man should do a full day's work for a day's pay. Some of the guys slow down fifteen minutes before quitting time." No one would say that of me on this job. Each day the work got easier as my body adjusted to the routine. Mentally, I was climbing a mountain, and there was satisfaction in knowing I would make it. I was on cruising speed. Every day I did this until summer ended and it was time to return to school.

That fall my father took my brother and me to a Knights of Columbus luncheon. Men were talking, and someone asked my father about the boys standing near him.

"Are those your sons?"

"Yes, Don and Bob." He indicated which of us was which.

"Hall," he mused. "You guys look pretty solid. Did you work at the McGarry project on the underpass?"

"Yes, we did"

"Boy, that must have been some effort. I heard you hit hard pan. Could clear out only a few inches a day. Had to use jackhammers."

"Yup . . . true."

"I know the foreman. He told me about it. Said you were two of the best workers he ever had."

I glanced at my father. He seemed pleased but didn't say anything—compliments were hard to accept—but it was enough for me.

The Lumberyard

IN 1882, MY GRANDFATHER, Mathew Hall, came to America from southern Germany. He was nineteen. At first he did gardening and took special business courses at school. He learned to keep meticulous records. Then he worked ten to twelve hours a day, six days a week, mostly in the woods and in a sawmill north of St. Cloud. He made $1.75 a day and was able to save much of it. His boss, C. A. Gilman, who was also lieutenant governor of the state, liked Mathew. "I would have trusted him with every cent I had in the world," Gilman is quoted as saying in a county history, published in 1915.

When Mathew was twenty-five, Gilman sold him five train-carloads of dimension lumber and encouraged him to set up business in St. Cloud. Mathew leased a vacant lot and began his business. Two other sawmills were operating in town. "Competition makes you strong," he was quoted as saying in *Mississippi Valley Lumberman* magazine in 1943. "But if you do the right thing you'll always come out right in the end. My suppliers are fair to me and I am fair with my customers. We buy good materials, sell them at a fair price, give good service. What more is there to it?" In time he bought the leased site on a four-year installment basis.

In 1928 he bought the coal business across the street from his yard and moved his office into the large brick office building that came with it. "The coal business kept him going during the depression in the 1930s," his son Herb would say in later years. "Everyone needed heat."

Mathew's four oldest sons all worked with him in the business. The youngest of the four was my father, Marcellus. Mathew seemed old to me all the time I knew him. He died in 1958, one month short of ninety-five. I was twenty years old. He went to work every day until the final year of his life. When asked why he didn't go to California or Arizona for the winter he said, "Why should I? Here are my friends. Here is my enjoyment." He would go to Duluth occasionally during the summer pollen seasons. He felt the cooler air and pine trees helped his asthma. He had no need to go farther.

I feel I know Mathew's work habits from my father's. Apparently, they were similar. Mathew trusted Marce with customer responsibilities, Mother said, an assignment he knew was important from his early days working alone. Marce would arrive for work early, stay late, show personal interest in customers, talk as long as they wanted to talk, laugh at their quips, help them make decisions, deliver quality merchandise, and in all, be fair. He enjoyed the work.

My father revered Mathew. So did I. But I was young, reflecting the aura around me. Later I learned to see my father in the same approving light. I think it came from realizing that I simply liked my dad. I liked to be with him. I liked the person he was, and because of that warm feeling I was able to overlook any faults he may have had. His actions always seemed to spring from a base of goodwill and therefore mistakes were not intentional. I suspect my father felt the same way about his father. He always spoke of him respectfully, almost reverently. My eyes water when I think about them. They're gone now, as is the simplicity of their times.

The lumberyard still stands just north of downtown, where it's always been, but it's changed. In my youth there was the brick office building, garages for trucks, and coal sheds along the railroad tracks. Across the street spread over half a block were various lumber sheds with alleys between them, the original wood frame office, and an old schoolhouse used to store building materials. Down the far alley, between lumber piles stood a pump with a tin cup on top, free to anyone in need of a drink. Bums got off the railroad and came over for a drink. It seemed like a regular stop. Sometimes they would stay and work long enough to pick up enough money to buy whiskey, then move on. At home in the evenings, Dad would marvel at how hard some of those men could work, and then he'd wonder why they simply drank and moved on.

One block east of the yard, the business owned a barn that held up to a dozen delivery horses used in an earlier time, and a caretaker's house. By my time, a half dozen trucks were in use, but Tom and Sandy, two old draft horses, were still stabled in the barn. One Sunday dad lifted me up and set me on Sandy, the gentler horse. Then he set my brother Bob on Tom, but held him tightly, for Tom was skittish. I held myself in place by tightly gripping Sandy's mane. The horses were old then, used only for an occasional parade commemorating pioneer times. Dad told of their final days of service.

"After the Armistice Day blizzard in 1941, there was so

The wagons are loaded with lumber for a new barn, ca. 1916.

much snow, the streets were blocked. Nothing moved for days. But we had to get coal to people's houses. These two horses could step through the drifts and deliver the coal. They got their picture in the paper." And there I was, sitting astride an aging hero, hoping she wouldn't move and cause me to lose my balance. I felt like a boy prince, important but scared. I imagine now that Grandpa just couldn't get rid of those horses, the last of a line, horses who raised his reputation for service to such a special level. He owed them a decent retirement. Economics and emotions are often at odds.

Grandpa never learned to drive a car. My brother Richard tells me he tried once, but lost control, drove over a curb, and never got behind the wheel again. But Grandpa did have a car, a 1941 Lincoln in my time and before that a Cadillac. His son Herb did most of the driving. Grandma didn't drive either, of course; she was a woman. When I learned to drive, Dad often asked me to take his car and bring Grandma to morning Mass. I would do so, then cruise around town and have a forbidden cigarette before returning the car to my father.

Grandpa owned two satellite yards in the nearby towns of Cold Spring and Albany. He also owned various rental houses. They were haggard, unpainted, weather-beaten, some of the worst-looking houses in town. One still had an outhouse. I'm told he acquired most of the properties from people who couldn't pay for the lumber. I don't know if he was harsh in demanding payment, but it was certainly obvious he didn't spend an additional dollar fixing them up. "They are an embarrassment," said Mother. "He could at least give them a coat of paint."

I always felt comfortable in the lumberyard because I was family. It was a piece of me. I felt I belonged. The other workers paid attention to me. Whose kid was I? Did I want to help? Once, when coal was being delivered to a house near ours, Bob and I did help. We were watching, and then asked if we could get up in the truck. "Sure," the workers said, so we climbed up and helped shovel as much as our nine- and ten-year-old bodies could handle. Coal was heavy, and half of each shovelful spilled to the ground as we stretched to lay it in the chute. Soot flew in the air, stuck to our sweating skin, and covered our clothes. We felt good about it; we were workers. The men smiled, knowing we would go home filthy with coal dust, and I suppose they thought it was fair. After all, it was part of the family work, and the business wasn't just conducted in the office. When we got home, Mother was sort of amused, but she made us get in the bathtub before we touched anything in the house.

When summer grew long and we were too much in the way, Mother occasionally sent Bob and me to the lumberyard with simple instructions. "Go ask your father for money for a haircut," she said one day.

"I don't want prickly hair down my shirt," I argued.

"It won't hurt you," Mother said. "Now move along," and she fairly pushed us out the door. So Bob and I walked the seven blocks from our house to the yard to get the money.

As always, Rita, the bookkeeper-cashier, met us with a big smile when we entered the building. "And how are the twins?" she said. We were often dressed alike, and we were the same size.

"Fine."

"Pretty good."

A customer waiting nearby looked us over. "Who's the oldest?" he said.

"Me."

"And who is the toughest?"

I looked away, embarrassed. "Him." It was the truth. Once Bob got to be five years of age, he could take me down.

But we enjoyed the attention.

Father was waiting on a customer, as always, during our unannounced visit, so we sat in chairs by the front window until he finished. We knew we were not the most important people in his life under those circumstances. When he finished with the customer, he started to approach us. But then

another customer came in the door and Dad waited on him.
We watched. Then another customer came. And still another.
Three quarters of an hour went by.

"It's not fair, we were here first," Bob said, and I agreed
with him.

Finally Dad gave us his full attention. He explained that
customers come first, and when we told him the purpose of
our visit, he entrusted us each with seventy-five cents for a
haircut. Then he said, "It's the end of the month. I want you
to pay the electric bill. You'll be going downtown anyway. Do
you know the Northern States Power building on Eighth and
Saint Germain?"

"Yes," Bob said. "It's on the same block as our school."

"Yes," I said.

"Well, go to the back of the building and pay the lady. If
you're not sure, just ask somebody."

"I get to carry the money. Bob, you do the asking," I said.
Mother had always told me I was the responsible one. Carrying money was a responsibility, I thought.

"Why?" Bob wondered.

"Because you're better at talking."

"Oh, OK," Bob said.

For being helpful, Dad gave us each a small booklet. "See
these calculations on the back?" he said. "The carpenters use
those in their work." I treasured that booklet and when I got
home put it with my other valuables even though I couldn't
understand the calculations.

It was all rehearsed, I realize now. Mother and Dad had
planned ahead of time to keep Bob and me busy for an entire
afternoon. And we learned things: we learned by watching

how the business operates; we learned how to talk to people; we learned how to pay bills. I want to do work like my dad does someday, I thought at the time. I want to pull out my billfold stuffed with money and tell my sons to go pay bills.

Later that summer Dad came home from work excited. "There's a rabbit's nest in the long grass on the boulevard at the lumberyard. One of the men discovered it while cutting the grass. I guess we let it grow too long." As soon as supper was over he took us in the car to show us.

"Where is it?" I asked, as we pulled along the boulevard.

"It should be right here," Dad said, but he had to look around awhile to locate it. Then he got down on one knee and parted the grass. "Here it is." Sure enough, in a shallow hole, covered first with grass and then mother's fur were half a dozen naked, pink, blind squirming babies, right there on the Seventh Avenue boulevard. The lumberyard wasn't all work, I realized; it was sometimes pure enjoyment.

When I got older I noticed advertisements for the "Mathew Hall Lumber Company" in the previews before a movie. I got so I would watch for them. That's my Grandpa, I thought, advertising right up there for the whole town to see, and my Dad works there. At church I would read the records of people's contributions and look for Grandfather's name, then my father's. I would compare. Grandfather's was more than most, but not on top. Father's name was in the middle someplace, as were his brothers'.

Some people thought we were rich because we were in a family business. Sometimes I thought we were rich, although we didn't live that way. Grandfather was a saver and a provider.

When they got married, he built a new house for each of the sons who worked for him. But he did not give them much in salary. Over time, Mother struggled with this. She felt there wasn't adequate money to properly take care of her family of five children. Every time she needed something special, Dad had to ask Grandpa. Finally Mother took it upon herself to tell Grandpa they needed more money. They got it, all right, and so did the other sons who worked for him, but Mother was considered pushy. It was not praise.

Sometime in the 1950s the workers at the lumberyard formed a union and went on strike. Bob and I and some of our cousins were brought in to help work. People driving by called us "scabs."

"What's a scab," I asked.

"A strikebreaker. Someone who takes a worker's job," my cousin Andy said. Then he added, "But we're family. How can we take a job from our own business?"

Dad hated the idea of a union. They insisted on defined jobs. That meant he couldn't tell a worker to make a delivery to a customer in need of special attention if it wasn't the worker's specific job. "Your own business and you can't tell the workers what to do," he said. "Hnnhh."

That's right, I thought. A boss should be able to direct his workers.

The next day I saw pickets. Guys with signs saying how little they made per hour: $1.15 or something like that. I was embarrassed. It didn't seem enough to raise a family and some of these men had worked in the business for over forty years. I myself might make eighty cents an hour, and I was a teenager. I mentioned my concerns to Dad. He bristled a little, then told me how Grandpa would take care of employees when they needed it, how he would keep them on sometimes when work was slow just so they could have an income. He thought they should trust Grandpa, just like he did.

But Grandpa was of another era. The wages of the present were simply too high in his mind. After a week of negotiations, adjustments were made and the strike was settled. Matt Rader's son told me many years later that his dad didn't like working at the lumberyard, didn't think he was paid what he was worth. I was taken aback. My dad thought the world of Matt Rader. I had assumed Matt would hold Mathew Hall and the lumberyard in the same high regard.

From the outside, Grandpa's family seemed like one from the storybooks: grand old man with a successful business, sixty-five-year marriage, ten children, four sons working with him. Another son, a lawyer, was elected speaker of the house in the Minnesota state legislature; the other became a priest. His daughters were educated and stylish. One married a physician, another a dentist, another an insurance man, and one a publisher. The family was nearly sufficient unto itself. No marriages came apart. No strange personalities emerged. Grandfather worked until his final days.

Once he died, however, difficulties at the lumberyard began to surface. I had moved away by then, but heard the stories from those around.

Al, the oldest son, became president at the age of sixty-five. For whatever reason he picked on Erv constantly. He tried to

The Mathew Hall family and their home on 13th Avenue North, St. Cloud.

assert authority over Herb and Marce. None of this worked well; all the brothers had been used to making their own decisions under Grandpa. Lawrence, the lawyer, asked to have his son work in the lumberyard. Al, Marce, and Erv wanted their sons to work there also. Some sons were more qualified than others. More than one liked after-hours drinking too much. The brothers argued about who should get the jobs and what was best for the business. One son was let go. Hard feelings smoldered, unresolved.

One day Marce decided to paint the main counter where he worked. Al came out of his office and said, "Who told you to do that?"

"I told myself to do it. That's who."

"I'm in charge here," said Al.

Marce erupted in a fury. "Do it yourself then." He threw the brush to the floor and walked straight into Al, backing him up against the wall. "I'm tired of taking your guff. And so is Erv; the way you treat him is a crime."

"I'll decide what we paint."

"Fine," said Marce. "Run the damn place yourself." He left and slammed the door.

For two days Marce stayed at home, pouring himself shots of whiskey. Never before had he engaged in marathon drinking like that. Mother suggested he settle down, but there was no managing him. On the third day he sobered up and returned to work. He told the others he wanted to get out. He wanted his money. He would take the yard in Albany where his son, Richard, worked. It was a twenty-mile commute and he could keep on working, something he wanted to do anyway. The lawyer and priest both came to visit Marce on the weekend to ask him to reconsider, to remember it was family. "No, it's better this way," he said. "I can't work under that arrangement." The brothers then agreed that Marce could have the Albany yard.

In time, affable, laid-back Erv, Al's verbal punching bag, had a son step forward with a down payment to buy the business. Al agreed to sell. Herb, with no children of his own, became a mentor. The Albany and Cold Spring businesses were eventually sold. The St. Cloud yard carried on the name.

Erv's son, Jim, the third generation, ran the business successfully. He is now retired and his three sons are in charge. That makes four generations and a history of more than 115

The family business in 1889 and 1989.

years. I'm still proud of the business. I'm proud that it's successful. I remember the early years when I was young and everybody paid attention to me because I was Marce's son and Mathew's grandson.

Marion

LOIS, MY GIRLFRIEND NEXT DOOR, grew up to be a fine young lady. But when I returned home from boarding school one summer I noticed she was six feet tall, still bearing a pleasing smile but beyond reasonable sight lines for me. I was five feet seven and done growing. Also it didn't look like I was going to be able to live on a farm. I was heading for college and from there into business of some kind. I suspected it would be hard to find a farm in a big city, and indeed, when I eventually moved to Minneapolis, I found that to be true. So I had to keep looking for something to fit my developing adult circumstances.

Church, I discovered, is a good place to size up girls. As they're coming back from communion you get to see their faces straight on. You get to see how they carry themselves. You can almost tell whether they're arrogant, self-assured, comfortable with themselves, timid, maybe even fun, just by how they behave as they come down the aisle and retake their seats. For sure you can tell if they're really religious.

I spotted Marion that way one weekend when I was home from high school. First, there were her two sisters, pretty; in fact, one of them was a St. Cloud queen candidate. They were of interest, but a little old for me. Then came Marion, since families sat together. I don't remember her father or mother. I learned later that her father was an usher, so he wouldn't have been sitting with the family, but his being an usher would have been important to me at the time; it meant he was a good Catholic.

Marion walked with elegant posture, her head held in an assured manner. She had a clear wholesome face, dark wavy hair, and dark eyes against fair skin. Bright eyes, in fact. Her mouth was modest, thin-lipped, but red with lipstick and framed by cheeks with a slight rose tint. Those bits of color suggested a warm fire inside. She was not too tall and not too short. Since she had a coat on, I couldn't assess her contours, but in church you're not supposed to dwell on such things. You're supposed to pretend you don't notice. In the Catholic religion we were led to believe that sexual attraction took care of itself. A good marriage was based on common values, self-sacrifice, good character, and being blessed with children. Sexual compatibility was assumed. I learned from my religion teachers that love was an act of the will. By that definition you could, and in fact, *should* love your enemies. The church didn't say you had to marry your enemies, so presumably married love was an act of the will and then a little extra . . . (ahem) pleasure. We didn't discuss that part, except that getting too involved before marriage was a serious sin. We were warned at length about infatuation and how temporary it was. Anyway, Marion looked real nice.

I saw her again a few years later working in a popcorn wagon at a city dance. I bought popcorn a couple of times to get a good look at her. She looked just fine again, pleasant too. Since I got the right change, I assumed she was good at arithmetic. But how the hell do you talk to someone who's stuck inside a popcorn wagon with customers coming and going at the only open window? If we could dance, I thought, I could learn more about her, see if she's graceful, see if she'd follow my lead, consider her body a little better up close. But it didn't happen.

Four or five years later, when I was working in Minneapolis, I stopped home for a Thanksgiving visit and in the evening went to a place called "The Bucket," a roadhouse you might call it, just north of St. Cloud. The place served 3.2 beer, had a small dance floor with booths around the edge, and a jukebox that played for a nickel. The beer was cheap, probably twenty or twenty-five cents a glass. I know that if you had a dollar you could have a decent, but frugal, time, maybe even buy a girl a beer. Two bucks was very comfortable. Prices were not as cheap as in my dad's time, of course; he said a nickel could get you a glass of beer *and* a sandwich at Waibel's downtown when he was young.

My cousin Mary Sue was at the roadhouse and with her was Marion. Wow, what an easy introduction. Marion and I talked a little, she laughed at my jokes, I asked her to dance, and she accepted. We were connecting . . . finally.

When the place closed at 1 A.M. we went with another friend to his house to have a final drink or two and listen to music. Then I took her home. On the steps to her front door I tried to kiss her, but she retreated a little and offered me her hand. I smiled and kissed her hand. I understood her behavior. She had been raised with the same guidance I had: Don't kiss on the first date. Let things develop. A man doesn't respect an easy woman. But I knew she had a good time, so I asked if I could call her next week. "Yes," she said. "That would be nice."

Within weeks I decided Marion would be a good candidate for marriage. I was twenty-three and ready for it. It wasn't a revelation or a logical thought process. It just seemed right, all the time. I had no illusions about perfection, for I was aware of my own imperfections. I was grateful that she accepted me as I was and I, in turn, found it easy to accept her just as she was. I liked being with her. I thought she was pretty. And she was fun. And she was smart. And she was neat and clean. And she smelled nice. Once she mentioned that her hips were a little larger than average. "Good for childbearing," I said, thinking it was a nice, family-oriented comment, just a touch risqué. She frowned a little, and I learned to be more sensitive. Whether she saw imperfections in me I don't know, for she didn't mention them. The closest she came was to tell me she was disappointed in me, once, when I drank too much at a party. I marveled at the discretion of that remark, for the truth was I was flat-out drunk. I had driven over a curb on the way home.

After three months of simple dates, Marion invited me to her college prom. When I arrived at her house, she opened the door and I saw such regal beauty I almost lost my breath. There she stood in a maroon velvet dress with a satin sash and a scoop neckline. She wore a simple crystal necklace and matching earrings. They were hand-me-downs from family weddings, she told me later, but that evening they adorned her in simple, elegant glory. I stared.

"I'm so lucky,"

"What's that?" she asked sweetly.

"You look beautiful."

I had my hair combed back neatly and wore a deep green suit with a vest and a simple white shirt and striped tie. I felt like a dandy, myself. That evening we danced in innocent joy. I pressed her close to me and felt her body. I'm with this beautiful girl, I thought. She feels warm and cooperative—how could I be any happier? And what does she feel, I wondered, the buttons on my vest? But I could tell she seemed happy, whatever her thoughts. So, gently I pressed my cheek to hers and she did the same. My reverie, it seemed, was mutual.

Marion's mother encouraged us to be romantic with each other. She knew, I'm sure, that Marion would never be a loose girl, so she wanted to help a little in the other direction. She dimmed the lamp next to the davenport in the front parlor so that it would be a natural place to sit when I brought Marion home. Marion would invite me in and then we would sit in this shadowy cove and enjoy smooching at length after dates. I loved it, and Marion seemed to be happy, too, when I was around. To me that was proof of her love.

I wrote letters to Marion weekly and in them I made dates. "I'll pick you up at 7, Friday night, and we'll go do something. If we can't think of anything we'll just walk down Main Street and look in shop windows. Love, Don."

"I have tests on Thursday and a paper due on Friday, but I'll be ready when you come. I like walking down the street. Who knows, it might lead somewhere. Love, Marion," she wrote back.

We went bowling, to dance halls, to each other's house for dinner. Sunday mornings we went to church. Together we went to communion. It meant we wanted a sacred as well as a romantic relationship. We were in love, behaving just the way we were supposed to, on our way to marriage. But Marion had to finish college first before we considered anything serious. My feelings for her never wavered. One evening I was on my way to pick her up after a party with a bunch of her girlfriends. The coolness of fall had settled in, but it was fresh and beautiful out. Instead of knocking on the door, I thought, I should stand on the lawn and sing a love song. I should sing the old campfire song:

> *Tell me whhhhyyyy . . . the stars do shine.*
> *Tell me whhhhyyyy . . . the ivy twines*
> *Tell me whhhhyyyy . . . the sky's so blue*
> *And I will tell you . . . just why I love you.*

Or I could sing the World War I ballad that talked about leaving it all behind, finding a spot to call our own—"a sweet little nest"— and letting the rest of the world go by.

It would be wonderful, I thought. She'd love it. And her girlfriends would, too. I really should do it. In fact, I should sing "Some Enchanted Evening" like Ezio Pinza, or better yet "It's the Loveliest Night of the Year" like Mario Lanza. Yes, that's it. I should be like Mario Lanza. I should sing on the lawn to Marion. But what about the high notes? I wondered. How would I handle them? I might squeak and warble, and then everyone would laugh. But, still, it would be wonderful. They'd know I meant the best. They'd see my heart exposed to the world and wouldn't be able to help loving it. But then again, maybe someone would say, Who do you think you are? Mario Lanza? Maybe I shouldn't do it. It could be embarrassing.

I stopped in front of the house, waited for a minute, then got out of the car. The lights were on in the house and I could see a living room full of girls. I envisioned myself standing in the middle of the lawn. A streetlight provided backlight. It would be beautiful. But I can't do it, I said, finally. I don't have the voice. I went up the steps to ring the doorbell and ask for Marion. She came to the door and smiled sweetly.

Damn it all, I thought to myself. I should have sung that song. It would have come from my heart, not my lungs, and everyone would have known my sincerity. Instead, I said, "Hello, Marion."

In the cold winter before graduation I began to talk about marriage. I told Marion the special sacred words, "I love you," and then I added, "I think we should get married."

She said she loved me too, but she was not sure about marriage. Marriage was so certain and final. One should be very certain about marriage. She wanted to know for sure if we were having the *real* love we learned about in school. And how could she know it was not just infatuation?

I answered that it was real, I was sure of it. I had no doubts. More than that, I was eager to get married. Marion felt she needed a little time. She was twenty-one years old.

She talked to a priest and told him of her fears and doubts. She told him of our courtship, now into its second year. She told him of our compatible personalities. But how could she know, she asked him, if it was real love? And what if she made a mistake? The priest listened and then told her everything was OK. She should get married, he said, and she would be happy. When I heard about it I was nonplussed at this visit with an expert about our private romance. To me marriage was obvious, and there was no reason for delay. But I respected her need for affirmation, and when she told me his answer, and therefore her answer, I began shopping for a ring.

That spring, on Good Friday evening, after supper, I stopped at Marion's house and suggested we go for a ride. She agreed, so I quickly drove out of town searching for a place of privacy. I pulled off the road at some gravel pits and parked facing the moon. I was so eager I just reached in my pocket and pulled out a ring.

"Here," I said. "I love you." Marion admired it. She looked at me. I saw her eyes glisten with tears. Beautiful brown eyes, floating in happiness.

"Try it on," I said.

She slipped it on and gave me a kiss, and then we threw our arms around each other.

"Let's go ask your mother if we can get married." Marion looked at me, smiled, and nodded. So I started the car and drove to her mother's house. I wanted to get this job done, and I was enjoying it.

"I'd like to marry Marion," I said to her mother. "Would that be OK?"

"Sure," she said, and smiled to the ends of her face. "Come in. I'll pour some wine and serve some cake. I'm very happy you're getting married. Come in. Come in. George would be proud. This is exciting." (George had died two years earlier.)

We set the wedding date for December 29, 1962. Marion would be graduated by then and teaching high school. Had we gotten married sooner she would not have been hired as a teacher for fear she would "have a baby," as they said—"pregnant" was too frank a term. So Christmas break was the best time. "Nobody gets married in the middle of winter unless they have to," one of Marion's aunts said. But we didn't care. We wanted to get married, even though we didn't have to.

In the fall of that year Marion had an overpowering bout of fear. She startled me with it one night as we were sitting in the car kissing and talking. "I'm not sure I can go through with it," she said.

"What do you mean?" I said. "What's the matter?"

"I couldn't sleep last night." She paused. I looked into her face and waited for more. "I might be going crazy. I can't think straight. You don't deserve somebody crazy." And she began to weep. "I'm scared."

I took her hand. "I don't understand," I said. "I'm pleased to deserve you. You're wonderful. I love you. I don't have any doubts. You're a very good person."

She pulled out a hanky and blew her nose. Tears rolled off her cheeks. "I guess I'm just afraid."

"Don't worry," I said. "I'll take care of you. We'll be happy." She continued to cry softly as I looked ahead out the front window, searching for answers. I squeezed her hand. What can I say that might make sense? I wondered.

Then, I turned authoritarian but in a gentle voice. "Marion, we're engaged. We're going to get married. It will work just fine. It worked for our fathers and mothers. They probably had doubts, too. We'll be happy. It's the right thing to do."

"Well, I hope so. I just have this creepy worry. I don't have any doubts about you, I love you, but I worry about marriage. How can I be sure? How are you so sure?"

"I don't know. I just know that I am." As if to prove it I kissed her easy on the cheek.

"If you're 98 percent sure, you're sure," I said. "Nobody's 100 percent sure. Everybody has doubts if they think about something long enough." Her sniffling receded and we relaxed again in the quiet. A police car drove by. There was no action here. We were alone by the side of the street.

"Let's get married," I said.

"OK," she said. We kissed on the lips. I knew she meant it.

We got married in St. Mary's Church, a High Mass. That meant three priests singing the ceremony. We wanted God to notice. Marion looked as beautiful as she did the day of our first prom, only this time in white. She had a crown and veil. She might have been the Virgin Mary, the standard of heavenly beauty by our Catholic values.

I was nervous.

"Do you take this woman to be your lawful wife?" the priest asked.

I fluttered with nervous pride and excitement inside. Yes, I answered. I hoped the tone was right, but I suppose some nervousness showed. When her turn came, Marion smiled and answered yes, too. I could see that she was also nervous and happy.

Our family and friends all came to the wedding, except my brother Bob, who was serving in the army in Korea. I felt like I betrayed him. We were so close as youngsters; I should have waited for his return. He would have been my best man. He sent a tape, however, and recited Shakespeare's sonnet:

> Let me not to the marriage of true minds
> admit impediments. Love is not love
> which alters when it alteration finds,
> or bends with the remover to remove.
> O, no! it is an ever-fixed mark,
> that looks on tempests and is never shaken;
> it is the star to every wand'ring bark,
> whose worth's unknown, although his height be taken.
> Love's not Times's fool, though rosy lips and cheeks
> within his bending sickle's compass come;
> love alters not with his brief hours and weeks,
> but bears it out even to the edge of doom.
> If this be error, and upon me prov'd,
> I never writ, nor no man ever loved.

He was Laurence Olivier that day, in voice, anyway. But I could not wait for Bob when I was making my plans, because marriage had a stronger grip on me. It was so strong that our wedding was being held on a day when the temperature was below zero. The sun was shining, though, and it was a bright, crisp, beautiful day. Rosemary, our guest from New York, was flabbergasted to see a car driving across Pleasant Lake outside the window of our reception hall. Instead of Bob, Marion's brother, Tom, served as our best man. When we got in the car upon leaving church he pulled out a flask of brandy and passed it around. Brilliant, that Tom. It was just what we needed then. I think Bob would have done the same.

At the head table Tom entertained everyone with witty comments and gave a toast to his baby sister. Another sister, Ginny, brought a carpenter's saw to cut the cake. Larry from Minneapolis gave a toast to me, that I might always steal, cheat, and lie.

"That is, steal away from sin," he said, "cheat the devil, and always lie next to your wife."

About five o'clock Marion and I jumped into my little Volkswagen to drive to Minneapolis. The engine chugged and choked, and the car lurched and lurched again. With each hiccup Marion and I bounced forward, then back. A group of men stood on the curb laughing. "He'll figure it out," someone said. But Marv Berg, my buddy from college, knew better. "Stop," he said. "I'll show you." He opened the engine hood and reinserted a couple of spark plugs. I laughed and thanked him for saving my wedding night. As we pulled away tin cans rattled behind the car. A few blocks down the street I ripped them free and we were off . . . to a honeymoon suite in Minneapolis.

We had dinner first and asked the waitress for a recommendation on a nice drink.

"Would you like a quick rush or something slow and sensuous?" she asked.

"A quick rush," I said.

*Don and Marion, with Pleasant Lake in the background:
December 29, 1962.*

"Slow and sensuous," Marion said. The waitress left to fill our order.

"How did she know this was our wedding night?" We laughed to each other. "However did she know?"

"I think she could see it on your face," I said.

"Yours too," my wife said.

Behind The Scenes

MOTHER HELPED ME GET MARRIED. She was always concerned about my love life. Maybe it was because I had acne in high school and was very self-conscious about it. About the only way I could get comfortable with girls was to loosen up with beer—something Mother did not recommend . . . er, tolerate. But she would encourage Bob, who was much more adept socially, to fix me up on a double date. This was my *younger* brother, who everybody said got the good looks. It's a little embarrassing to have your younger brother fix up a date, but I needed the help and I appreciated it. I really did like girls. Mother would tell me to simply go out and have a good time. Without saying so directly she was also telling me that there were girls out there who would like me and I shouldn't worry about my complexion.

During college in Milwaukee, things got better. With some medical treatment the purple scarring on my face was removed and I gained confidence. But Mother kept up her concern. When I came home on school holidays, she would ask if I had any dates. "Yes," I answered once. I had finagled a date because I knew the question would come up.

"And what was her name?" Mother said.

"Judy Marinelli," I answered, and it was the truth.

"Marinelli," Mother said. "You don't want to marry an Italian woman; they all get fat when they get old."

So I didn't marry Judy. Instead, I kept experimenting with a date here and there.

After college, when I started dating Marion, a St. Cloud girl, Mother was again paying close attention. After my second or third date, I mentioned to her that I was going to meet Marion after church. That is, we would both go to the same Mass, but we would meet on the steps afterward. I would stay cool, I thought, and not show the whole world I'm ready to get serious. A man should saunter, not rush, into love.

But Mother said I couldn't be so cavalier, so male. If I had asked Marion to meet at church, then I had to do it right and pick her up at home and take her to church, and then sit with her during Mass. This is what I was trying to avoid; it seemed so quick and serious. But Mother didn't suggest; she declared what was right. As I thought about it, I liked the idea, though, and if Mother thought it was proper I decided I had better do it. I wanted everything to be right with Marion. So we got serious; that is, we let ourselves be seen in church together.

A few weeks later, Mother had another gentle command. "Ask Marion if she remembers wearing your underwear," she said, trying unsuccessfully to control her mirth. I hesitated and considered that this was my mother speaking, the one who was always telling me how to behave, and Marion and I were just getting to know each other. Marion was very proper. She had only let me kiss her hand on the first date. We were up to the lips now, and I was pretty sure the underwear stage was a long way off.

"So I should ask Marion about wearing my underwear? What's this about?"

She wanted to be sure Marion and I were getting along well before she brought up this little story. But by then, we'd had a few dates, and she couldn't wait any longer. It just burst out.

"Well," she said, "after the war, Marion's mother and I were shopping downtown and we visited a little. We talked about how hard it was to find clothes because of the shortages. Marion's mother said she needed underwear for her two girls and she just couldn't find any."

"Uh, huh." I listened attentively.

"So I told her my boys had just grown out of theirs, and she could have whatever she needed. She accepted. So Marion must have worn your underwear when she was four or five years old."

As I thought back, I recalled underwear of my youth. There was one item I particularly didn't like. It was one-piece, sleeves down to the elbows, legs to the knees, and it had a button flap in the back. I'm not sure if it had a male opening in the front. I think not, but it had buttons down the front. It was made for warmth, not ease of use. We dressed heavier in those days; buildings had lots of cold drafts. Anyway, that was the underwear we gave away.

So I told Marion and she remembered, with reluctance and some discomfort. Over the years I grew to like this story for its quaintness. It described an earlier way of living, a time of shortage and thrift, and of sharing directly with friends.

Marion has never grown fond of it, however. Something about dignity, I think.

Mother was pleased Marion and I were going together. Our parents knew each other well. The women were both in Christian Mothers, a church organization I heard mentioned often, but never learned what they did. Our fathers both helped in Boy Scouts. Both couples were in a square dance group together. And my father and Marion's mother had attended grade school together. Marion and I did not meet each other until we were older because she was three years younger than I, and she lived on the south side of town and I lived on the north side. Also, I went away to high school and college. But once we met, Mother wanted to nurture this developing romance.

When the right time came, I told Mother I was ready to buy Marion a ring, or maybe it was Mother asking when was I going to buy her a ring? I'm not sure. I told her I thought I could spend a hundred dollars. I only had eight hundred dollars, and I was intent on accumulating more so that I could invest in stocks and get rich—for both of us, of course. A man was supposed to provide. Mother said spending a hundred dollars wouldn't do; I had to spend more, to show proper respect. Again I listened to Mother and found a ring for four hundred dollars. It cut my assets in half and deferred my financial goals immeasurably, but I liked Marion a lot, so I bought the ring. It was a simple diamond ring, but it has helped hold us together for more than forty years. Marion has reminded me that the money I spent turned out to be a good investment. She's right. And, too late now, I thank my mother for the advice.

Our Home

HOUSING IS A MAN'S RESPONSIBILITY, it seemed to me in the early years of our marriage, and that suited me fine because I was concerned about how we spent our money and what style we chose. I wanted shelter at a reasonable price and with character, if there was such a combination. Also, we should live close to my work to save commuting time. Ten minutes, maximum. Marion was homebound, now, in the apartment we were renting, about to have a child. When the baby came, we would have to move because children were not allowed in the building. Knowing that, I set out to find new space for my new family.

Within weeks I was able to report to Marion.

"I found a real nice place, so I rented it. An upper duplex in south Minneapolis. Near Powderhorn Park. Only a hundred dollars a month."

"Sounds good," said Marion.

"There's nice woodwork throughout the living room and dining room. Built-in buffet. A cut-glass window." I paused to let her enjoy the mental picture. "An enclosed front porch. Two bedrooms. I think you'll like it."

I was a young, but not very good, imitation of my father.

"Look at the detail in those hinges," he'd say. "They don't make 'em like that anymore. Doesn't pay." And, gazing at a window: "Eight lights in a sash; that means this house was built in the early 1900s. And here, see, they had a pass-through window from the dining room to the kitchen. That was for the maid. Lots of people had maids back then, that's why they had back stairways." I would listen when he spoke about those things and imagine myself owning such a place someday. But for now we were renting.

"What's the kitchen like?" asked Marion.

"The kitchen? The kitchen?" I repeated. "I don't know. There was one ... and a pantry. But I forgot to pay attention to what it was like. I really don't know what it was like. Sorry."

Marion was cooperative anyway, and we moved into the upper duplex. The nondescript kitchen turned out to be functional, but not very attractive. Dirty-looking linoleum on the floor. Peeling linoleum on the counters. We had to buy a refrigerator. Nevertheless, it had the necessary sink, stove, and counter space for Marion to prepare her usual imaginative and delicious meals.

But I didn't stop looking. These were temporary quarters. My parents were pushing us to buy a house. They even offered to give us the down payment, something they wanted to do for all their children.

"A house is a good investment," my father insisted. He had seen the rise in values since World War II and thought it would continue. His father had built a house for him when he got married in return for his services in the family business.

He felt pleased to pass on the favor. Marion also wanted a house, a place she could decorate as her own. And my mother had an opinion: she felt sorry for Marion stuck at home in a blue-collar rental neighborhood and thought she deserved her own place as well. Having studied finance, I thought we should put our money in stocks. But I couldn't stand against this trio, especially with the down payment inducement.

If I am to buy a house, I thought, I must learn about houses, even the kitchens. So I went looking at houses almost every weekend. When I found a good one I took Marion along to see what she thought. If we had serious interest I asked my parents to come to town and look it over also. We looked at many houses.

One day my parents were in town, and we went to see some offerings newly placed on the market.

"I think it's a good buy," my father said as we left a stucco, gabled, three-bedroom house in the Washburn neighborhood. I agreed it was a good buy, but I thought it was ugly. Painted woodwork. Worn, mismatched carpeting. Small rooms. I couldn't see the possibilities, except that they would all cost money.

"It's in a good neighborhood," Mother said. "Best thing we ever did was move from our old neighborhood. Nothing but old people there. It was too hard to make friends." She was identifying with Marion, stuck in that upper duplex I thought was so nice.

What the hell, I decided. It *was* a good buy, and the $3,000 down payment was a gift; we might as well buy the house. Marion agreed. So we bought it . . . for $18,700. Again I thought of it as a temporary decision, maybe a five-year stay.

It was not the house of my imagination, or Marion's, although she was pleased to be in it.

All the while we lived in that house, I kept looking for a bigger, better, older, and more beautiful one to buy someplace in the adjacent neighborhoods. Often Marion and I would spot a prospect that looked just right from the outside. Then, when we got a chance to look inside, we would be disappointed. Poor floor plan. No backyard. Too pricey. Something would be wrong.

Meanwhile, we set about upgrading the house we had bought. We removed the carpets, sanded and finished the floors, and had the paint removed from the woodwork. That transformed the living room and dining room. We had the kitchen remodeled, and the bathroom. They then looked fresh and clean. We upgraded the plumbing and wiring. We painted or repapered every wall in cheerful bright colors. In the yard we planted shrubs and flowers and put a trellis with morning glories and a window box along the side of the garage. These framed a comfortable patio space in the morning sun, just right for lazy Saturday morning coffee or afternoon cocktails with the neighbors. We repainted the outside trim. With each step the house improved, until eventually both Marion and I were quite proud of it. Our kids made friends in the neighborhood and liked the nearby schools. The house felt right. It looked good. But still the spaces were small, and it was tight on the lot. We wanted something bigger, older, a little grander.

One day we found a very promising prospect—from the outside, at least. It was new on the market, two and a half blocks up the street, half-timbered, stucco, brick trim, small window panes, two small dormers facing the street from the third floor. It gave the impression of an English country home on the outside. We walked up the front steps and through the front door, hopeful, but knowing we'd been disappointed many times. Beamed ceilings. Dark satin woodwork in the living room and dining room. Fireplace. Built-in buffet. A very good start. To the south, French doors and a sunroom, something our current house did not have. The kitchen, good size, but needed work. A small bath on the first floor ... and a study with bookshelves to the ceiling. The floors were level. We looked out the back door. Very large yard, unusual in the city. Nicely landscaped with shrubs and trees. Some big elms. Double garage. Then back inside we went and up the stairs. Stained glass window on the landing. Four bedrooms on the second floor. Bathroom needed work. Then to the third floor. Two more rooms with dormer windows, ideal for our teenage sons. The central stairway had a cabinet on each floor designed to hold a fire hose, a unique historic touch. The house, we were told, was built in 1910. We played it cool, asking questions methodically. How was the wiring, the plumbing, the furnace? What were the taxes? But I only half listened to the answers.

Once outside Marion and I almost embraced with excitement. This was the house we'd been looking for; we both knew it immediately. This was the kind of house Marion lived in as a teenager and on through college. This was my grandparents' house.

It was 1981, a tough year for housing, but we sold our house for $91,500 and bought the new one for $162,500. Both prices pleased us. We were home, at last. Our "starter" home had

The house of our dreams.

served us sixteen years, but this would be our real home. The first one was a project; this one, a love affair.

I invited my parents to come see our new house. There had been no need to have my father review it beforehand. I now had full confidence in my own judgment.

"What did you buy this for?" Dad said as he entered our new house. "These old houses, you can't get parts for them." He walked into the south room bright with sunshine. "Windows don't fit tight. They're drafty." He tapped the outside walls. "Are they insulated? Most of these old houses aren't insulated properly." He continued checking details. "If you buy a new house, you don't have much to fix for twenty years. Lotta upkeep in these old houses. How much are the taxes?"

I smiled. I knew Dad was trying to help. When I was young he had told me that during the Depression people lost homes because they couldn't afford to heat them, couldn't afford the taxes, couldn't afford to keep them up. I figured he was worried. So I told him I sold some stock to reduce the mortgage. He nodded, as though that were a smart thing to do.

"We bought this house simply because we liked it," I said after he had inspected it. "Look at the woodwork. Feel this door . . . solid. Did you see the backyard? There aren't many backyards that big in the whole city." I told him I learned to appreciate these things from him. I used to listen when he talked about the old days. He seemed surprised. He apparently didn't realize he'd made an impression on me with his earlier commentaries. It was now apparent to me he appreciated both old houses and new, but for different reasons. He had spent his adult life selling people material for new houses. He thought they were more practical. But he had always shown an appreciation for the quality and workmanship in old houses. He must have thought he was talking to himself when he made comments about the quality of old things, that nobody was listening. "Well, I suppose it's OK," he said finally, almost cheerfully.

Two months after moving into the new house our great friends, Wittas and Perkins, held a surprise housewarming for us. All of our friends and family were invited. Dad was in a wonderful mood, showing everybody around. "Look at the grain in that wood. Those old carpenters used hand tools to do this. Can you imagine? You can't get that anymore. And look here, eight lights in the sash. Tells you when the house was built."

Mother-in-law

MARIE STEINWORTH EGERMAN* fit the central Minne-sota, German Catholic pattern almost perfectly. Very simply, she believed in hard work; she let the priest and nuns de-fine her moral life; and she relished parties with family and friends. It was a simple, rewarding life, perhaps not much dif-ferent from her ancestors' lives in Germany.

Her father was a stonemason. "He drank too much," she said. Accordingly, she felt her family was lower class and crude. She also did not think herself smart. She attended only eight grades of school, one of which she had to redo. But the nuns who taught her seemed to like her, and they helped her have a healthy self-respect and a rigid certainty about proper behav-ior. She smiled easily and liked to make conversation. Upon finishing school she got a job as a department store clerk.

At the age of twenty-two she married George Egerman, six years older than she, who was working at the St. Cloud post office. George was a man of thrift and moderation. He enjoyed music, dancing, and reading, and had a calm manner about him. Although she was slightly taller than he, she felt

---

*Originally spelled Steinwart Egermann.

elevated by him. "He was refined," she said, "and handsome." Together they had eight children. Their marriage was permanent, absolutely permanent. There was no questioning the marriage vows in their culture, and most likely neither felt the need—maybe the occasional escapist wish, but never the need—to get unmarried.

George died of cancer shortly before I met the family. Marie, by then, was fifty-nine. My observations on her earlier life are based on listening to conversations between her and her children and the talks I had with her alone when Marion was busy. She would gossip about people, but in a sympathetic way. She was also starkly honest about things. Once, when asked how she kept from having even more children, she said, she sometimes had to tell George to roll over and forget about it for a while. I admired her strength of character. She was a very religious, good woman, but not overly pious.

My parents-in-law, Marie and George Egerman.

Maybe my attitude was bent in her favor because I was a son-in-law. She spoiled all her sons-in-law with lavish approval. We were guests always. She made us feel honored simply for being men.

Her children she did not spoil. Standards were administered by directive and example. Work came first, then play. Do your duty. No pretensions. Don't waste money. Go to church. Do what the priest says. Other people come first. Don't think yourself important. Be grateful. Get a job. Keep it. These attitudes were imprinted deeply on her children, except for Tom, the most creative one. She found it hard to relate to Tom, even though his artistic genes probably came from her side of the family. Interspersed with the demands for proper behavior was a bubbling happiness. She had a round, almost pumpkin face, with a bright smile. She liked jokes. Bathroom terms were funny, sexual ones were not. "Pants up, and skirts down," she told the older girls in a simple admonition before dates.

Next to her family, of course, her special pride was her hair, which was red. She had good taste in clothing and she liked flowered prints that complemented her autumn hues. Finding an attractive dress at a bargain price made her joyous. It had to be on sale, though, to bring full joy, for vanity could not overcome thrift. Only in later years did she wear pantsuits—to be in style. I thought she never looked right in them. She belonged in a vivid, colorful dress.

Although very careful with money, Marie instigated a bold financial move when she and George bought the large, yellow brick house at 707 - 7th Avenue South in St. Cloud, two blocks from the small, three-bedroom house into which they had, until then, squeezed eight children. It was 1945, the fifteenth

straight year of depression or war. A bank had acquired the
house in foreclosure. It was square with a short hip roof like
a doughboy's helmet, but across the front stretched a screen
porch that gave it personality and some additional form. Inside, lots of personality showed—beautiful oak woodwork,
pocket doors, and a central stairway that divided two parlors.
There was also a dining room and an informal sitting room,
and in the rear a kitchen, back porch, and back stairway. The
upstairs, split with a central hallway, had five bedrooms and
a bath. With two sons returning from military service, Marie
thought the additional space was important.

But George was reluctant. The price was four thousand
dollars, and he was afraid it was too much of a financial reach.
So Marie reassured him. She said she would take in roomers
for extra money.

They bought the house, and when the older children married
and moved out she did take in roomers. The house became a
matter of great pride for both George and Marie. I'm told he
spent many hours decorating, maintaining, and improving it.
But for Marie there was another element at work. The house
at an earlier time had been owned by her well-to-do uncle, a
higher-class citizen in her mind who had been unable to hold
on to it. Lowly Marie, in buying the house, had moved up in
class. She laughed at the thought of it. But she never showed
airs; that would be wrong.

Almost every Sunday while dating Marion I was invited
for noon dinner at that fine house.

"Now you sit in the living room," she said. "Dinner will

be ready in a little bit. Marion, get Don a beer." I would lower
myself into the velvet Victorian davenport, place an arm on
the curved wooden armrest, and look across the room and
into the front parlor. The furnishings seemed appropriate
for such elegant space, colored wallpaper and Victorian-style
chairs, sofas, and tables. Marion brought me a beer freshly
poured in a fluted glass with half an inch of foam. I felt like a
duke, marrying into quality, upper-class St. Cloud.

When dinner was ready, I was invited into the dining room
for Marie's Sunday specialty, chicken baked in a flour crust
with lots of salt and pepper and other spices. Plates of corn,
peas, pickled beets, relishes, a salad or two, fresh buns and potatoes and gravy were brought to the table. "Now go ahead and
eat," she said. "There's more in the kitchen." I was a man, she
seemed to think, and was expected to eat, because men had big
appetites and if I didn't eat enough it was because I was reluctant to ask for more. I liked the man part. Fortunately, I was
young and could eat half a refrigerator of food. By doing so,
I thought she would know that I liked her cooking. "It's very
good," I said. "Especially the chicken. You make it special."

"Well, go ahead, have some more. Now don't be bashful.
There's plenty more where that came from," and she'd pass me
the plate, unbidden. So I would eat another leg. It was truly
special, but I didn't dare say so again. I had already loosened
my belt two notches and there were no more to go. "Marion,
get Don another beer. His glass is empty." In this room I'm a
Bavarian baron, I thought. Then she served apple pie with ice
cream and peach pie with ice cream. I could have both. "Now
don't be bashful."

Afterward the women cleaned up, and I was invited to stretch out on the couch.

"Well, I should help a little," I said. "I know how to wipe dishes."

"Oh, no, the girls and I will do them. You just sit in the living room. Now, take it easy. You work all week."

"Are you sure? I'm good at wiping, you know."

"No, no, no, that's the girls' work."

"Would you like me to carry out the garbage when it's ready?"

"No, no, one of the boys will be along later. They'll do it. Virg always stops by on Mondays. I'll ask him to do it."

I couldn't win this discussion, and of course I didn't want to contradict the dear lady, so I went into the living room and sat on the couch. When the work was done we played canasta on the dining table.

At sundown I said I had better be leaving. "My car is in back. I'll go out through the kitchen. Perhaps I should take the garbage with me."

"Oh, no. Bob or Dick will come by later. They usually do. One of them can take it out."

"It's no problem. I can take it."

"No, there's no need for that."

"Well, OK then, I'm off." I kissed everyone good-bye. "Auf Wiedersehen."

"Well," she said, "if you're going by the garage . . ."

"I'll take the garbage," I said. "It makes me feel good. Garbage and I are compatible. Oops, no offense, Marion."

I don't know how many times we went through this, but eventually I figured out that I should carry the garbage out without asking. We had our signals mixed up. She served me extra food without my asking, and I was asking about things I should have known could be done. I took no offense, though, for I knew her intentions were generous, extremely generous.

Marie loved preparing meals and loved company. In later years, when her children moved on to their own lives, Marion and I would sometimes visit and find she had chicken dinner prepared just in case somebody stopped over. She would break into a happy laugh when we came in the door. Preparing and serving meals fulfilled her.

But with advancing age her cheerfulness waned. She suffered from arthritis, which caused a limp, and her eyesight began to fail. She went to daily Mass and began to pray that God would take her. It may have been the only thing she asked for herself in her whole life. At the age of eighty-one, she died in her sleep.

My throat tightened and tears watered my eyes when I heard of her death. I was at work and had to find privacy to mourn. I had called her "Mother" and kissed her every time I saw her once Marion and I got married. Mother-in-law jokes never amused me; they were about somebody else. I realized I had great feelings for this woman who treated me so special, who was always happy to see me, who wanted to feed me and make me comfortable, who loved me just for . . . I'm not sure . . . just for marrying her daughter, I guess. I don't think it was the free underwear after World War II; we never discussed it.

Good Advice

SCHOOL WAS ENJOYABLE, I realized as I finished college. Why not continue? So I decided to go to graduate school at the University of Minnesota and major in finance.

As an undergraduate I had learned the basic principles of investing and portfolio management—diversification, market timing, scheduling maturities, dollar cost averaging—and they all seemed like useful tools. I thought I was already educated in the basics; now I would be refining things. But my new finance professor, Ben Sutton, had other ideas.

He arrived the first day, ascended the two-step platform in front of us and sat on the desk, dangling his legs before us. With arms supporting him, he leaned forward as if starting a conversation, but began to lecture instead. No notes.

"Diversification downgrades a portfolio," he said, and paused to get our attention. "There is one investment, probably a stock, that will do best over the next ten years. All other holdings will downgrade your performance. Why have an average investment when you can have a superior one?"

Hmmm, I thought. This is interesting. The logic is irrefutable. I guess he's telling us to be selective. Be *very* selective.

"Market timing . . ." He paused in a way that told us he

was introducing another subject. ". . . doesn't work. There is
no analytical tool to tell you when to get in at the bottom
and out at the top. To be successful at this you better major
in psychology and somehow learn to read the minds of all
other investors. But you won't be successful. Many investors
got caught in 1930 when the market went up 50 percent, and
they thought it was safe to reinvest. They thought 1929 was
the top and 1930 was the bottom. Over the next two years
the market went much lower. It is very hard to tell either a
market top or a bottom, and it requires a miracle to recognize
both. What you *can* tell is if something looks like a good value
based on its own cash generating possibilities, but you won't
know if the overall market is at a bottom."

He moved on to the next subject. "Scheduling maturities. Bosh! Since 1890, 60 percent of all corporate bonds got
called before maturity. Twenty percent defaulted. How do
you schedule results like that?" Then he looked around to
give us a moment to digest this information. The class was
silent as everyone was filling their notebooks trying to keep
up. This was too good to forget. Every word was important.
Soon everyone finished writing and looked to him for more.
He launched into another item of financial convention.

"Dollar cost averaging—you know about that, don't you?"
he asked rhetorically, then helped us remember. "That's investing a fixed dollar amount each period so that you buy
more shares when the price is down and fewer when it's up."
We nodded appreciatively. "Well, that's lazy, mechanical investing. With ability and good information you can do better
than dollar cost averaging."

Then he opened the class for discussion. I was speechless.

He had demolished the cornerstones of portfolio investing that, until then, I thought sensible. What he gave us instead was the directive to gather good information and then trust ourselves to make the right decisions. And not dilute them.

He's talking to me, I thought, a guy who used to memorize baseball statistics and then make judgments on them. I could go out and find that superior stock. In fact, I'd like to. It would be a game of intellect and it would be exciting.

After college I got in and out of stocks, never finding the perfect one or even one that would go up a little, for that matter. This went on for a couple of years and I was behind a few hundred dollars, but with each trade I gained experience. Then I got lucky. I bought Control Data, the revolutionary computer company whose stock price was in a swoon at the time because of competitive worries. I knew little about the company except that it made a very fast computer that sold for less than IBM's comparable model—twice the speed at two-thirds the price, if I remember rightly. Scientific laboratories and universities were buying them. Shortly after I made my purchase, the issues concerning competition lifted and the price of the stock lifted as well. I also bought Polaroid, which was then pioneering instant photography. Both stocks tripled within three years. The dollar amounts were small but the successful results gave me confidence that this was a game I could win.

Later, when I went to work for Control Data, I got a second chance to take advantage of a drop in price. This time there were real product performance difficulties. Customers stopped placing orders. I bought 100 shares at around $25 a share. Within two years the problems were corrected, and the stock went to $150 a share. Now I had $15,000, decent money, I felt. I sold and invested in another one of what I thought would be Ben Sutton's perfect investments, a small start-up company. This had the potential to really grow into sizable money because I was in with the founders at a very reasonable price. But potential is not reality, I learned. The stock did nothing for ten years. Further, it was hard to sell because the market was so illiquid and I was a member of the board and was expected to hold on to my shares. My investment was stuck. Not gone, just stuck. For most of those years I was unable to do any meaningful investing.

In 1976 another chance came along. Seymour Cray had started a new company, and it was selling shares to the public. I knew of Seymour Cray, as he was the brilliant design engineer who had created Control Data's successful machines. He was about to build supercomputers, but this time in his own company. It looked like there would be no serious competition. Control Data, the most probable competitor, had hedged its bet, and was a shareholder in Seymour's new company. But the company was still in a start-up phase; there was no revenue and the future was very speculative. The stock was priced to come public at $16.67 a share. Because of strong demand, I was unable to get any at that price, so I placed an order to buy a small amount on the opening trade, hoping it would be close to the offering price. My order filled at $25 a share, the high for the day. I felt like a sucker, like I may have been the only one who paid such a high price for the stock. Nevertheless, I followed the progress of the company. In time, Seymour announced he was planning to build four machines, each priced at $10 million. Surely he wouldn't build them, I thought, unless he felt quite sure he could sell them. So I calculated the sales price, the gross margin, the amount likely to be spent on research and development, on marketing and on general administration, then a tax rate, and I ended up with projected earnings per share. Once all this happened, I reasoned, the stock would be worth $40 per share. Meanwhile, the stock had dropped to $17 a share. This looked to me like another chance.

Thinking back on my earlier Control Data investments, I thought about how I might have made more money if I had been able to invest more. I had always been puzzled by stories about people who started with nothing and quickly became millionaires. How do they do that? I wondered. How do they get something from nothing without building the slow tedious way from scratch? As I read and studied I learned that the secret was OPM, other people's money. It was even referred to that way. Get other people to lend or invest with you and make the combination grow. It gave you leverage. Of course, if it didn't work, it could lever you backward, so a person had to think it through carefully.

Borrowing for a good investment wasn't a bad idea, I thought; everyone borrowed to buy a home. The house was collateral. Few people worried about not being able to pay off the mortgage. I felt the same about investing in Cray Research. I was sure it was going to work. I had the numbers all worked out in my head.

I talked to my wife about it. I told her I thought we should borrow money and buy the stock. I said it wasn't much different from a businessman borrowing to buy inventory that he was quite sure he could sell at a profit, or a farmer borrowing to buy seed and fertilizer so he could plant a crop in the spring and sell it in the fall. I also pointed out how everyone borrows to buy a home. Sure, there was risk, I said, but I wouldn't borrow more than we could somehow repay—perhaps with a second mortgage, and I reassured her that I was not a reckless, compulsive gambler. I would only do what I thought was prudent. If we lost and our kids had no money for college, they would find a way. They could get jobs or student loans or, perhaps, scholarships. We should not just hoard our little money so that we could pay for college education. We should invest instead, and maybe send them to better schools someday. Marion didn't like the idea of borrowing money to buy stocks, but she trusted my arguments and she agreed to try it. The stock was still around $17 a share.

The next day I called my father and told him I wanted to borrow some money and buy Cray Research stock. I knew all about the company, I said, and I would split the profits with him. He said that wasn't necessary. He would lend me the money at interest. I bought more stock at $17.50 a share.

The stock moved up to $20 a share. I bought some more, this time with money borrowed from a margin account at the brokerage firm. Then the stock went to $28 a share; I bought more. Always, I felt, we had the wherewithal to repay, if necessary, although it might set us back a long way. My analysis of the numbers showed the stock was worth at least $40 a share. I was confident.

One day I was talking to the president of a small Minneapolis brokerage firm and I explained to him my full analysis—the number of machines, the price, the profit margin, and therefore projected earnings per share. I said the stock was worth more than it was selling for, and that he should buy it. He thought about it carefully and then he said, "What if Seymour dies?"

Dies? *Dies?* I was crestfallen. I hadn't thought of that. Indeed, what if he dies? Seymour was essential to the success of the company and he was unique, a genius, hard to replace. If he died, Seymour would go to heaven, but our stock would go to hell. We had borrowed all this money against the stock. What if he dies, I thought, and I couldn't shake the worry.

At supper that evening I raised the question to Marion, "What if Seymour Cray dies? We would be in tough shape," I said. "I had overlooked that possibility in my earlier analysis." She was busy with supper and the kids and didn't seem too concerned. It was my worry, she must have thought, and she was right. I went to sleep that night, thinking, what if he dies . . . what if he dies . . . dies . . . diez . . . zzzz.

The next morning a new thought was in my head. What if he lives? I literally jumped out of bed and said aloud, "What if he lives?" Where did we get the idea he was going to die? The odds are 99 to 1 that he will live. And then think what will happen. Our stock will be wonderful, and I decided right then to no longer let such morbid thoughts control my thinking. I envisioned success.

Three years later, the stock went to $100 (adjusted for splits). We were ahead over $100,000. This was getting to be real money. We were in a position to help our children with college. I sold the stock, repaid the loans, and invested in other things.

That same stock subsequently became worth $3 million.

No matter. Marion and I had taken our chances and won. We were satisfied. No one can see the future for certain, and Professor Sutton had said no one can pick the top. Besides, there were always other opportunities. The professor's principles remained the same. All I had to do was pick another opportunity.

The Truth

AT THE AGE OF TWENTY-FIVE I decided to be a stockbroker. I had been working as an investment analyst in a bank trust department, where I received a thorough understanding of the market and of the major investment choices at the time. I felt it was time to move on. I wanted to get out of the corporate setting and into a more individualized setting and, I hoped, earn more money. Perhaps, in time, I could develop a business of my own as my grandfather had done. A stockbroker is largely in business by himself.

Although not on the same professional level, a stockbroker's work seemed similar to a lawyer's or a doctor's. From a thorough understanding of a large base of information, the appropriate particulars are applied for an individual client. I felt I could do that—in the field of investments. As a youth I had memorized baseball statistics, thinking it was important, until one day I asked myself who, besides me, cared if Johnny Vandermeer pitched two no-hitters in a row in 1938? Of what use was such information? And I stopped accumulating it. But I learned from that behavior that I was organized and analytical, and I decided that, in the future, if I were to immerse myself in a field of knowledge, it would be in something useful.

I had been introduced to investing in my sophomore year in high school. My father owned a few stocks, and when our family came to Minneapolis to shop for clothes he would stop in at Paine Webber Jackson and Curtis and visit his broker. He took me along. I was intrigued by the activity: the ticker tape printing out the latest prices—*tat, tat . . . tat, tat, tat . . . tat, tat*—throughout the day, while women in slacks read the tape and recorded price changes on an elevated chalkboard that extended the length of the room. Brokers sat at desks and watched the chalkboard, then talked to their customers by phone. It seemed like a game that a keen observer with good judgment could win. At my father's urging his broker supplied me with numerous booklets and brochures about various aspects of the market. I appreciated the help, but I did not have the background or vocabulary to really understand the material at that age.

My mother stirred my thinking about investments, too. When I was a freshman in college she gave me an autobiography of Bernard Baruch, the great investor of the early 1900s and occasional adviser to presidents. His accounts about searching out and finding successful investments made the process real for me. I was inspired to try and imitate his skill. No doubt my mother anticipated this when she chose the book for me.

So, at the age of twenty-five, with my preparation completed, I was ready to be a broker. I went to J. M. Dain & Company and asked for a job. I told them of my experience and that I had been a member of the Minneapolis Jaycees and as a result I knew a lot of young professionals and businessmen who would want my services. The president of the firm seemed to like what he heard and was about to hire me, I believe, but he wanted me to take a little test they used to help predict success. I agreed to take the test, thinking it would be as easy to pass as any college exam.

A week later, the president called. "We can't hire you," he said. "The test shows that you do not fit the profile of a successful broker."

"Hmm, I'd really like to work for you. I think I'd be a good broker."

"Sorry, but we have to trust the tests. If you wish to explore this further you can talk to our psychologist. He advises us on the tests."

"Well, yes, I think I'd like that. It would help me understand."

The psychologist reviewed the test findings. "You're interested in too many things. As a result you're indefinite about what you want to do with your life. The company's afraid they'll train you and then you'll leave for another job." He paused and sorted through the papers on his desk. "This isn't true of their successful brokers. The profile is clear. They're highly motivated by money. They like to sell. Your profile is indefinite."

I said the tests were probably right, that I *was* uncertain about the many choices in life, but that I had nevertheless decided to be a broker. I *wanted* to be a broker.

"I believe you," he said. "It's just that the tests show otherwise. We have to believe the tests. A lot of science has gone into these tests."

"So how do I deal with this?" I asked. "Tell them what they want to hear?"

He looked at me with empathy, then nodded slowly—yes.

I was dumbstruck. I felt he was telling me to circumvent his own tests. All my life I had been told to tell the truth. My grandfather had built his business on a reputation for honesty. My father had stressed the same virtue many times. The priests taught me to confess all lies, even little ones. I remembered a discussion in grade school in which someone asked the teacher, a nun, if it was OK to lie in order to save a million lives. She said, no, as hard as the choice was, lying was wrong. I had absorbed very thoroughly the importance of honesty. How could this man in a business suit, sitting across from me, who seemed sensitive, not arrogant, who was respected in his profession, tell me to lie? I thanked him for his advice and went away to think about it.

He was right, I decided: life wasn't black and white, true or false. There were nuances to be acknowledged. When you withheld some unpleasant news, when you hedged on an undesirable commitment, when you flattered to gain good favor, when you spoke in approximations, you were in that gray area between truth and falsehood. I had done some of that and I wasn't necessarily a liar. I decided I had been interpreting the rules too rigidly. They didn't fit reality. Life wasn't rigid. Life was flexible and sometimes even illusory. I had to loosen my standards.

So I went to the Smith Barney brokerage firm and applied

to be a broker. They liked my credentials and offered to send me to New York to be interviewed by headquarters, and, oh yes, in New York I would be given a little test . . . just a little screening test.

I was ready for them. I went to New York, had the interviews, and then took the test. It had tight, controlling questions such as, Would you rather read a book or go to a party? I might like to do both, but with my new insights I gave the answer I was quite sure they wanted. I would rather go to a party. The questions continued on, and soon the choices got tighter: Would you rather read a book or go fishing? Would you rather read a book or go to the theater? Would you rather go to the theater or go to a party? Would you rather fish or go to the theater? Always I gave the answer I thought they wanted.

After about forty questions, one of the interviewers entered the room. "How's it going?" he asked.

"Not bad."

"Everything OK?"

"Yah."

"You look worried and a little uncomfortable."

"Really?"

"Yes."

"I didn't realize it." I shrugged.

"Maybe it's because you're away from home. And you're wife's going to have a baby. That's probably it."

"Yes, probably."

"Well, carry on." He left the room.

Most likely, this intrusion was supposed to simulate the interruptions a broker gets during a typical day, but I didn't realize it at the time. I went back to my test. Would you rather fish or swim? Would you rather swim or read a book? Would you rather read a book or go to the theater? Hmmm. Didn't they ask that before? What did I answer? I couldn't remember, and I couldn't trust my instincts because I had given the answer I thought they wanted to hear. I was now in a labyrinth I couldn't escape. I worried that they were going to catch me contradicting the answers I had given just a short time ago. I got very nervous. I finished the test, thanked everyone, and returned to Minneapolis.

A few days later, the manager of the Minneapolis office called to say he couldn't hire me. He was sorry. He thought I had been a good candidate, but he had to trust the New York tests and I did not fit the profile.

I didn't ask for clarification. I was sure they didn't want a liar for a broker. I didn't want any further discussion. I had flunked the personality test a second time.

It was clear to me I was not broker material. I was better at analytical research work. So I looked elsewhere and soon gained employment in various financial capacities with Control Data Corporation. I stayed there thirteen years, then spent two years at another company, Data 100, until it was acquired. Then I had to make a career choice. At age forty-two I decided to reapply to the brokerage industry, this time doing research. I felt sure I would be good at doing research and writing brokerage reports. I had done very similar work at the bank fifteen years earlier.

I interviewed with R. J. Steichen & Company, a small firm, and was hired on an independent contractor basis to write research reports. After three months, the owner of the firm said to me, "Why don't you become a broker?" I hesitated, searching for an appropriate answer.

He continued: "The way you know the market and with the people you know, you should be successful. You'll make a lot more money as a customer man than in research."

"You think so?" I said.

"Yes. If you like, I'll send you to sales training class. I'm always looking for good brokers."

I kept my doubts to myself and accepted. I was excited and pleased about the opportunity.

I went to class as he suggested and became a broker. I decided to maintain the basic impulses learned in my youth and always try to conduct myself in a truthful way regardless of the consequences. I learned that a broker is more of a counselor than a salesman. The approach worked well.

Six years later another broker and I bought the firm.

Decisions

I WAS FULLY AWARE that any decision to get married was to be permanent and last for the rest of my life. There was no blurry optimism. It stood before me like a red-and-green semaphore. The marriage ceremony stated clearly that bride and groom must go forward "for better, for worse, for richer, for poorer, in sickness and in health, until death do us part." I had heard the vows recited solemnly by couples afloat in bliss many times when I was an altar boy, and I thought about their meaning. Would I be willing to stand by my wife in a time of illness that might go on and on and on? I imagined what it would be like, a life circumscribed by the needs of my partner, and then decided, yes, of course, I would be steadfast, and she would stand by me if I were the sick one, which was equally probable. It was a gamble, but it was fair. Almost everyone else lived under the same vows and they got along all right, or so it seemed to me.

When the time came to make the marriage decision, I realized that every choice I had made about my life up until then could be corrected if necessary. If I picked the wrong school to attend or the wrong neighborhood to live in, I was free to make a change. It made those decisions easier, even though in all cases the future was unknowable. But getting married was different, There was no escape, and I could not unburden that heavy understanding.

Nevertheless, when the time came it was not a hard decision. I was eager to get married. I wanted to stop going to bars, looking for girls and ending up drinking too much. It was an unfulfilling lifestyle and, as for finding girls, mostly unsuccessful. Without a wife, my passions were sin. I wanted to center my boiling, male heat on one, dear woman. And I wanted to have children. When I was a counselor at summer camp I thought of the job as a prelude to fatherhood. I liked being an adult to those children. Children were fun, I learned, and I wanted some of my own. When I found Marion, I was ready within weeks to make our friendship permanent.

I knew Marion would make a good wife. I had been told in school to recognize the difference between infatuation and abiding love, and had been warned to marry sensibly. Think of your lifetime together, we were advised in those classes. Infatuation will pass. Seek compatibility, seek similar values. Marion, I could see, had loving, sensible qualities, and she had the same values as I—not just Catholic values, although they were important, but other qualities like conscientiousness, a good nature, and a willingness to work. She would not spoil our children. She had the characteristics I noticed in responsible mothers and wives I knew. As we were dating and learning about each other, I asked her where she stood politically. I was searching for another compatible value. "I'm fairly conservative," she said. Good, I thought. She'll make a good partner for life.

Surely she would be a good homemaker (like her mother)

and, I assumed, a good cook (like her mother). I learned later that she was both, but my assessments were too modest; she turned out to be a marvelous cook. More than that, she had gone to college and she was a good student. I liked smart women. Ever since Marlene Reiter in the fourth grade, I had liked smart women. And her family was creative and musical. Some played the piano or the violin. The four girls all sang, often together in harmony. If I can be part of this, I thought, I will be happy. The girls were all pretty, each in a different way, while the four boys were hardworking and full of humor. One was an artist. We would have interesting children, my musings told me; Marion would provide the genetic qualities I lacked, and enhance the ones we had in common. Oh, it would be an exciting, satisfying adventure. We would make a home together, just like our parents, only better. We would have children and smile in satisfaction at their insights, their humor, their sense of adventure, their ambition, their goodness. We would have a family in which happiness spread like fission. We would be successful parents. Indeed, I learned later, there was truth to the dream. I learned that a good marriage and having children is one of the great blessings of life.

Politics was another matter. When I approached the voting age of twenty-one, I deliberated gravely about my tiny vote as though it would tip the scales of the republic. Would I vote Democrat or Republican, or perhaps something else? I would think it all through. Father Arnold, my high school social science teacher, made clear that every citizen had a responsibility to vote. "It is a privilege and a duty," he said, and because he was a priest it sounded like a moral imperative.

I accepted his laying on of duty, this rite of citizenship; in fact, I looked forward to it as much as I had looked forward to getting my driver's license just a few years earlier. Maybe my vote wouldn't carry an election after all, but it would be a personal declaration of my political values. It would be a considered, defensible decision. But before I declared myself, I knew, there was much to learn.

Early influences carried me in both directions. My parents had strong Republican leanings. Father was a businessman. He did not like unions. Democrats were the party of unions. Mother, for whatever reason, distrusted anyone in authority, and that meant for sure, Hubert Humphrey, our Democratic senator. She didn't like any know-it-all, in any field. When Humphrey's voice came over the radio, she would say in derision, "He's got all the answers. A program for everybody . . . giving away somebody else's money, just for votes." She didn't believe anything he said. Father would agree and shake his head in disgust, saying, "He talks too much." They didn't like Humphrey's "gang" either, "that McCarthy and Freeman and [Miles] Lord and Mondale. All looking out for each other, living off the government." Republican leanings? I guess it was a full ninety degrees off center, although they were critical of Republican politicians, too. They seemed to think the idea of political parties was corrupt, that people getting together to advance a specific cause was just self-serving. Politics should be simple: the will of the people, that's all. The less government, the better.

My uncle Lawrence, the lawyer and only politician in the family, was in the state legislature in the early 1940s. There was no party designation at the time, but he clearly drew his support from conservatives. I think he had moderate tendencies, however, as he was elected Speaker of the House, and I remember hearing him in later life defending the economic advancement of women.

The church and all of my religious teachers never betrayed a political preference that I noticed, but their lifestyles and beliefs reflected a conservative disposition. They mistrusted secular society and therefore most liberal ideas on social policy. Their lifestyle was clearly defined and righteous and they felt a need to conserve it, to protect it. A good Catholic farm family was some kind of ideal. Many of the priests and nuns came from such an environment. It was self-sufficient, protected from outside society, and it was right. It depended on hard work and trust in God. It was the good life, the holy life.

Yet there was a strong current of social concern. Mother and Father had sympathy for the unfortunate. They believed in restraint from greed; they believed in sharing. They believed in the church's mission of caring for the poor. They just didn't think there were very many poor to take care of. They didn't know them, not in St. Cloud. Oh, maybe a few. And maybe more in far-off lands. It was an ideal that didn't require much implementation. And in school we learned the concept of "distributive justice," the idea that the goods of society should be distributed justly. It was a moral issue. If it took the government to accomplish that, then the government should do it. And we learned that papal encyclicals had been written endorsing the rights of labor, including the right to organize, and certainly the right to a "living wage." Never did I hear a partisan word mentioned, but it sounded like a Democratic platform to me.

I was open to the possibilities. I was open to the right course, one that would define my values. My older brother Richard helped to clarify them for me one day when he described how he saw the difference between the two parties.

"Would you like to take care of yourself, or would you like the government to take care of you?" That was the choice, he said.

How easy, I thought. I am a man. I would like to take care of myself. I must be a Republican.

But I was not certain. I wanted to continue to study the issues. In graduate school at the University of Minnesota I began to hear arguments in favor of government. They seemed to fit the moral criteria my religious instructors had given me. They advanced the cause of distributive justice; they promoted the rights of working men and women, the rights of minorities, the rights of forgotten people, the very people Hubert Humphrey had been fighting for with his raspy, everlasting voice and his needling of the privileged class. His was a message of sharing, a Catholic virtue, it seemed, and he was a Democrat.

The 1960 presidential campaign was under way. My vote was important now, at least to me. I could have a direct role in electing one of the most powerful men in the world. Maybe he would thank me. I would be important. But it was serious business, and I must choose wisely. I must learn about the major issues and weigh them objectively. Every day in the fall of that year I read the front section of the newspaper as it laid forth the candidates' positions on major issues. There was much I agreed with on both sides; the candidates seemed to be similar. The differences were nuances, political salami cutting. I did not have a television in my room at a boarding house, so I missed the first television debate between Kennedy and Nixon. According to the pundits, I missed the decisive event in the entire election. It had nothing to do with issues and answers; it had to do with appearance. Nixon was sweaty and pallid. He looked nervous. Kennedy, meanwhile, looked relaxed and charming, they said, and it boosted him in the polls.

I thought this was nonsense. It was easy to notice Kennedy's good looks and I admired his easy charm, but these things were irrelevant. I wanted to make an objective evaluation of the facts, the positions.

One week before the election I was invited to my aunt Marie's house for dinner. She was my father's sister, living in Minneapolis, and she wanted to give me an opportunity for a home-cooked meal.

"Donny," she said, as we drank a cocktail before dinner, "whom are you going to vote for?"

"Nixon," I replied. "I think he's right on the issues. I would rather have less government than more," and almost without knowing it I declared myself a Republican. "Who are you going to vote for, Aunt Marie?"

"I'm going to vote for Kennedy."

"Oh, you can't vote for him just because he's Catholic," I implored. I knew she was a devout Catholic. One of her daughters had become a nun. "Aunt Marie, you're voting for him just because he's Catholic, aren't you?" I couldn't believe anyone in my father's family would not vote Republican. I felt sure her devotion to the church had distorted her thinking.

"No," she replied. "I like him. I just think he's the better candidate," and she smiled at how disarmingly simple her argument was. Had I known her better I would have understood. Aunt Marie had a very strong sense of social justice, I came to realize later. She believed in Democratic ideals. She was also a charming woman, and I might have understood had she said she had voted for Kennedy just because he was so good looking, but she would never have admitted to that. That would have been too sensual, and she was a good Catholic. I know as a man how I might have reacted to a charming and beautiful woman running for president, but I would not have admitted to it at the time either. I was a good Catholic, too.

Four years later, when the next election came up, civil rights had become a prominent issue. Gradually in my adult life, my eyes and mind had been opened to the profound injustice suffered by black people in our country. I read many books trying to understand their point of view. I attended civil rights meetings and rallies. I learned, slowly, that the problem wasn't just in the segregated South, it was prevalent throughout the whole country. Candidate Lyndon Johnson spoke boldly for advancing the cause of civil rights. Candidate Barry Goldwater said he was for the black person, but he believed in states rights. States rights! It was obvious that such a position would solve nothing. It was the states that had segregation laws on the books, and they wanted to keep them that way. To fix the problem would take federal action. Johnson and the northern Democrats would fix it. They would overrule the conservative Democrats in power in most of the southern states by passing federal legislation. The Republicans under

Goldwater would do nothing, because of a principle, states rights. I would vote for Johnson. Was I a Democrat yet? I was not sure.

Once elected, Johnson embraced the war in Vietnam. It was a stand against communism. To be weak in the face of communism seemed like political suicide for either party. John Kennedy had taken strong and dangerous positions against communism, and the country stood with him. Johnson continued that attitude. As the war escalated, opposition to it increased. Bobby Kennedy wrote an article in *Look* magazine that argued clearly that the war was misguided and wrong. It was definitive to me, a compelling case. Then Gene McCarthy challenged the president, a member of his own party, in the early primaries. The Democrats were making the case against the war, rightly, I thought. The Republicans, as near as I could tell, did nothing. They believed in another principle, this time supporting your country, or as Nixon later said, "keeping our honor," as though we were in some Mafia street fight. That was it for me. I became thoroughly Democratic. The Republicans, I thought, were wrong on the two major issues of our time, civil rights and the war in Vietnam. I was a Democrat, by God, and now I would say it out loud.

My parents thought I had lost my mind. They didn't think civil rights and the war were major issues. They thought we should support our laws, our government. But I was adamant. They were wrong. "When your country goes to war without sufficient reason, it may as well be called murder," I argued. "And because we live in a democracy we are all responsible. We are committing murder by killing people we don't know for convoluted, anti-Communist reasons."

My father became incensed. "Jerry is over there," he said referring to my brother in the air force. "He's not a murderer. He's fighting for his country."

"Well, maybe he's not a murderer, but our policy is murderous," I argued, my voice rising with insistence. "Why should we kill Communists? They're people just like us."

"Communists want to take over the world. They have to be stopped," he argued back. "We're helping those people over there just like we helped the Europeans in World War II."

"It's a civil war. Why should we choose sides?" I would not budge. I was certain of the morality of my position. Father walked away in disgust.

"I'm voting for McCarthy if he gets the presidential nomination," I said to my mother.

"McCarthy and Humphrey, that whole gang, they're all just politicians," Mother replied.

"Yes, they are," I said. "That's their job."

In time my parents and I reached a truce on politics. They let me alone, and I let them alone. But I did notice that when the Vietnam War ended, the Communists grabbed power in Cambodia and in the process killed close to two million people. *Two million people.* Now who were the murderers? I had to ask myself. My moral certainty turned to mush.

With age, I think both my parents and I learned that political issues can be very complex and that the answers are not easy. Overall, I'm sure we understood, although we never stated it, that no differences about politics or anything else for that matter should undermine our respect and concern and care for one another.

Marion eventually joined the League of Women Voters, an objective organization that studies and makes recommendations on issues. It is true that the organization consists mostly of upper-class, college-educated women, but they are fair. Scrupulously fair. Opponents would say they're all liberals, that they're so liberal they can't see their own liberalism. However, if they study issues and come up with answers that most often seem to favor big government, then maybe those are the right answers. My "fairly conservative" wife in time became more liberal than me. We changed in the same direction, but at different paces and amplitude. The transition was healthy for our marriage. And who could have foreseen it? We started with similar values and ended with similar values, but changed a lot in the process.

Death

SINCE THREE OF MY GRANDPARENTS lived into their nineties, as did both of my parents, I assume I will live that long also. It is not a soothing thought, however, since I know from observation that old age for most is not a serene rest at sunset.

My mother deteriorated slowly, became completely incoherent, and eventually died from Alzheimer's disease. It seemed to me a painful, inevitable trip to nowhere. And it took seven years. Had she possessed the power, I believe she would have cut that time at least in half. At the end she had to be fed, clothed, diapered, and carried. Although unable to express herself in any normal way, she greatly feared going into a nursing home and dying alone. In fact, she was terrified of it. We knew this from her emotional reaction—the tension and squirming when we first tried to move her—because by then there were no words. When she was finally moved there, she died in nine days, a shriveled, silent, skeleton in a fetal position, age ninety-one.

My aunt Marie lived to be ninety-nine, but the last eight years were in a rest home, where she was mostly bedridden with pain from cancer. Her daughters visited her every day.

My wife and I would visit occasionally, and Marie would be exhausted after half an hour. Her mind was good, and she certainly had time to talk with God, who must have been pleased because she was a good and holy woman, but there was no reversing her medical condition. Her inevitable death seemed to linger forever.

Most people would say my father had a wholesome, even enviable, old age. He could see, hear, walk, joke, and think clearly, though sometimes forgetfully, until the last day of his life. But I know he had annoying, discomforting, ongoing ailments. In his eighties he had a skin rash that kept him wrapped in warm blankets and in bed for months. The doctors did not understand it, and never really cured it. I think it was anxiety, the redirected energy of a man who knew he was slowing down and had a hard time accepting it. I deduce this because he had other anxiety-related difficulties like bloating and irregular bowels, which doctors could never fix. In his last years, although he could still walk briskly, he would sometimes lose his balance. Thinking sensibly, I suggested he use a cane.

"I'm not going to use a cane," he grumped.

"What are you going to do when the time comes?" I asked. "Just sit in a chair and say good-bye?"

"Yes!" he said. He didn't get the chance, however, and I think it was fortunate. He died suddenly, probably from a stroke, at age ninety-seven. He was sneaking an early-morning smoke, a small vice he reignited in old age, and he just toppled over. I'm sure he was ready to go.

When my uncle Herb passed the age of 100, I asked him if he had any advice, given a century of perspective. I valued his opinion. He was always alert, seemed to understand almost everything, and never spoke unless he was sure of himself; then he would summarize in one, cogent sentence. He had a thorough memory of many details in his life that he could recall even in his last days. He remembered when the income tax was initially instituted, as "temporary." He would not fake an answer or guess. If in doubt, he would say, "I don't know." His reply to my question was simple, striking, and I'm sure sincere. "Keep your religion," he said.

This was an answer I had not quite expected. Herb practiced his religion, but was not overly pious. I needed to explore his meaning. A nun who counseled the sick and dying in a local hospital had told me how people in old age gradually lose the normal functions of life—the ability to enjoy food and drink, friendship, sex, exercise, and regular sleep. At the end they worry about relationships—some bad that they want to reconcile; some good that they want to reconnect with—and they want to make amends with God. These thoughts came to me as I spoke with Uncle Herb. So I suggested, "Because everything else goes, and religion is all you have left, right?"

"Right," he said and felt no need to explain further. Religion to Herb was the teachings of the Catholic Church. At the age of 103 he died in a nursing home.

My grandmother Hall lived to be ninety-two. She had ten children, and the last one she raised to be a priest. She felt she owed God the service of at least one child. But shortly before she died, she had a worry. She asked that son if he had been happy being a priest. He reassured her that he had. Apparently satisfied, she died a few days later. I think that haunting question was her final confession, informal as it was. It seemed as though she were asking forgiveness if she'd done him wrong, even though, at the time she thought she was doing the will of God.

My grandfather Morris was sick in bed at our house once when I was young. I suppose he was in his late eighties. One morning he called to my mother, his daughter, saying, "I'm going to die, Icyleen," and there was fear in his voice. My mother, in her managerial way, said, "No, you're not. Now you just get up out of bed." And he did. He got himself dressed, came down for breakfast, and was OK for a few more years. He died alone in a hospital, age ninety-one, but I remember his fear of dying, this man who seemed both strong and gentle to me.

When I was in college, my father took me to visit his father, Mathew, then in the hospital. When it was time to leave, Grandfather implored my father, "Marce, don't leave me." My father lingered awhile and then said we had to go. Again Grandfather pleaded with him to stay. It was emotionally difficult, but finally my father and I left. I felt we were abandoning Grandfather. My father said there wasn't much more we could do at the time, and the rest of our family was waiting. Grandfather lived for a month or so more and then died at the age of ninety-four. I believe he had cancer of the stomach, and I was told he had nothing to eat in the last nine days of his life, only a little wine each day to keep him going. But I remember his tremble at death, this patriarch of our family.

I've thought about my own death. I've thought that when it foreshadows itself, I would like to accept it peacefully. I would like to make my good-byes and then leave. I would like to be very dignified and brave. I would like to be a good example for my children. I would accept the will of God.

One time I visited the gas chambers at a concentration camp in Germany. I saw photographs of bodies piled in a pyramid, as the last to live had apparently climbed over the others gasping for the final bit of oxygen at the ceiling. I wondered: if that were me, couldn't I just sit on a bench and accept the inevitable with dignity? But then, I thought, surely some of them must have wished for the same dignity, and they couldn't do it. The body must have a primal urge for life that overcomes all reason. If they could not do it, I could not do it either. I, too, would have been climbing up that pile for the last bit of oxygen. So how can I die in dignity? I know the stories of Saints Stephen and Lawrence, early martyrs who died by stoning and fire, but I do not understand how they so easily gave up their lives. I understand standing for principles and accepting the consequences. Jesus did that. Martin Luther King did that. What I don't understand is accepting death easily.

I fear death, and I know its coming is unpredictable. Genetics will not save me from a violent accident or deadly fever. Most of my relatives who did not live to old age died of cancer. I may have cancer in me now, although there is no obvious evidence of it. So I have prepared myself. If it happens soon, I tell myself, I will not feel cheated. I have made my choices. I wanted to get married and have children, and I have been rewarded generously. Our four children have been a source of immense joy. I wanted to live in a large, old home. I wanted a business that served people and brought community respect like my father and grandfather's. I wanted to do good.

I wanted to see Europe. If I had extra money, I would try to be generous. Now, as I review the past, I tell myself, I feel I've fulfilled my potential. It was an ordinary life, brightened by the lights I chose. If I die tomorrow, I won't feel cheated.

This acceptance was not easy to come to, however. As a young boy I thought a lot about dying as a saint. I learned that to achieve this at the highest level one should give one's life up to God, or at least to a high principle. I should be Gandhi; I should be Mother Teresa; I should be working among the wretched in America and screaming against poverty; I should throw myself against the bullets of war. I should die like Peregrine, the boy martyr from Italy. That would be saintly. That would be a life holy in the sight of God. Instead, I chose to work for money. Avarice, it might be called. I tried to squirm through "the eye of the needle." How could God see such a person as good? The question troubles me still.

But the Bible also says to use your talents, your God-given talents. My life shows I have not been given the talent to be a great saint, just as I was not given the talent to be a major league catcher like Walker Cooper. I am an ordinary person with a small talent for investing, a stockbroker. If I use money well and do not let it define me, perhaps I can live a worthwhile life—not a saintly life, but an average life, a life that will do no harm. I can be like hundreds of good people I've known who have surely been welcomed by God at death. I tell myself, then, that I am among those masses and because of that I can die in good conscience. If this is a rationalization, then God made it so, for God made me. God made the eagles, but He also made the sparrows, and He loves them both.

Having thought this through, I try now to stop worrying

about death. Instead, I tell myself to enjoy my days with grace and joy. When I was young, I lived in the moment. Every child does. Life unfolds like a grand opera, people singing all over the stage. It is so enchanting, there are no other thoughts. Then I grew older and learned to be responsible, to be on time, to plan ahead, to set goals, to accomplish something. I learned to live as an adult. Now I must relearn the joy of childhood. I must plan less, forgo achievement. I must psychologically give up the material things I've worked so hard for. I must learn to enjoy, but not rely on the pleasures of life. If I give them up willingly, they cannot be taken from me.

And I must know where I'm going. Uncle Herb said, "Keep your religion." But I believe he meant the refined essence of religion, not the rules of the church. I believe he meant I should keep a spiritual life, keep a conversation with God, keep a belief in the afterlife.

I'm sure he also meant that I should live a moral life. He didn't say it that way, because he didn't have the habit of explaining. If I had said it for him, I believe he would have replied, "Yes that's it." What he did make clear was that without such a spiritual relationship, there isn't much else.

I don't know if God approves of my thoughts. But if I die without fear, I will know He has sent me a miracle.

Tolerance

A GREAT SOCIAL REVOLUTION took place in America during the second half of the twentieth century. It's often called the civil rights movement, but that term is too limited. A larger and more inclusive name might be the evolution of tolerance. When the history books are written it should be the defining characteristic of our age. Our society has come from very prejudiced, judgmental attitudes into a comfortable acceptance of virtually all social behavior.

Consider the simple matter of clothing. Under the old conventions everyone dressed up to go to church, to go downtown to shop, and for sure, to travel. It was a matter of respect and of looking appropriate. Now, a person can wear a T-shirt and sweatpants to the most formal of concerts, or shorts and a tank top on an airplane, and no one passes judgment. You may not want to sit next to someone with uncovered armpits, but it's not appropriate to express your disapproval. It's the inner person that counts, society seems to have decided, not the clothes. Or, alternatively, sloppy clothes are cool. It's even OK to look unshaven and ugly, for ugliness is simply a personal judgment.

For another example, consider language. Virtually any word

can be used in the public domain without recrimination. Comedians are rampant with raunch. Newscasters use words like *condom* while updating us about what they believe is important in our daily lives. My remembrance of a generation ago was that any discussion of sex was completely inappropriate in public discourse, as was the use of words like *damn* and *hell* and the whole range of profanities beyond that. Teenagers a generation ago were asked to show respect to their elders; they now call them "you guys." Informal is cool.

But these aren't the important issues. The important issues are about how society treats individual people, about how it shows tolerance and respect for them and their personal needs. In this area the great divides of race, religion, sexual orientation, and gender have been bridged. Even ethnicity, but that was an easy one. My mother's comment about all Italian women growing up to be fat is now simply funny.

The older generation had different attitudes. "We used to call coffee *nigger sweat* in high school," my dad confided to me once. "And one day, coming home from grade school, my friends and I hollered *Christ killer* through the door to the only Jewish merchant in town." He was giving me facts that reflected the attitudes of his times.

In my own time the prejudices were still present. I listened as boys hung out on St. Germain Street in downtown St. Cloud.

"Gimme me that dollar you owe me."

"No, but I'll settle for seventy-five cents."

"Oh, you're always trying to jew me down. Gimme a drag off your cigarette, then."

"OK, but don't nigger-lip it like you always do."

"Hey, you fairy, I smoke like a man."

"You may smoke like a man, but you play ball like a girl."

"You're dumb as a farmer."

They laughed. Of course, they were friends, or else there'd be a fistfight. This was the bluster of young boys, the conversational edge of society's attitudes.

Jews were suspect in the minds of people I knew. You didn't want to do a business transaction with them. They'd get the best of you. And all Jews, apparently, were businessmen.

We got an ambiguous attitude toward Jews from the Bible. They were the revered prophets in the Old Testament, but in the New Testament they killed Jesus; this was quite clear. But I was mystified why society singled out Jews in modern times. How could you even tell a Jew? I wondered. I asked my mother once and she said, "Well . . . they have black wavy hair, and they have big noses. They like to show off. You can just tell." She had been a grade school teacher for one year near the Jewish area of north Minneapolis, and I thought she could help me understand.

I had learned at St. John's that you shouldn't judge a person by the color of his skin, and I observed that the community lived out that idea. A few of the monks and students were black, mostly from the West Indies, a place where the monks had missions. It delivered a message that made sense to me, that all of us were created equal, but it was a gentle message in the face of a powerful, different message from society.

I knew there was segregation in the South, but I had no idea how harshly blacks were treated. In fact, from the images I saw, they seemed to be happy. There was Uncle Remus in the movies. There were pictures of happy-go-lucky, water-melon-eating, cotton-picking, singing and dancing "darkies" in books and magazines. For the fun of it I had learned all of Steven Foster's doleful tunes when I was young—"Old Black Joe," "Suwannee River," "My Old Kentucky Home." They were not angry songs. They were about people's longings, not their hurts, and they were easy to sing. I could feel and understand the blues in them.

Blacks were not treated well in the North either, I learned. But I had believed that was because they lived in their own neighborhoods and looked and talked differently. I didn't real-ize that they were forced to live there, and that they had little hope of decent jobs in order to improve their condition. I had heard that Marian Anderson, the dignified black American who sang with the Metropolitan Opera, had to use the back door of the St. Cloud Hotel when she came to town to give a concert. Why that happened seemed mystifying to me. St. Cloud was as white as winter snow. Why ever could she not use the front door? Apparently, prejudice about proper social order took precedence over decency. When I moved to Min-neapolis I noticed that no professional business would hire a black person in a job with high visibility; it would have been too much of a threat to the social order. It would have created a spectacle.

The understanding of homosexuals in the days of my youth was ambiguous. It was easy to see that some males had effeminate interests. They would get teased, but there wasn't hate. Instead, there was mostly puzzlement. I couldn't imag-ine any sexual activity—except by "perverts" and I didn't know what they did either. Hell, I didn't know that much about heterosexual sex except in the abstract. Some girls, of course, were "tomboys." They liked climbing trees, playing ball, and other rough activities. This was not a problem so much as a difference. In fact, if they were cute their behavior could be appealing.

Society had negative stereotypes regarding Mexicans. Apparently because they took siestas they were thought to be lazy. In the late 1940s Peggy Lee had a hit song about Mexican indolence, sung in an exaggerated Latin accent:

> *The weendow it is broken, and the rain is coming ee-en.*
> *If someone doesn't fix it, I'll be soaking to my ski-een.*
> *But if I wait another day, the rain may go away.*
> *And we won't need a weendow on such a sunny da-ay.*
>
> *Chorus:*
> *Mañana, mañana, mañana is soon enough for me.*

Reflecting another harsh prejudice, Arthur Godfrey had a hit song called the "Too Fat Polka," which had the following brilliant lyrics:

> *I don't want her, you can have her.*
> *She's too fat for me.*
> *She's too fat for me.*
> *She's too fat for me.*
>
> *Oh, oh, oh, I don't want her, you can have her.*
> *She's too fat for me.*
> *She's too fat.*
> *She's too fat.*
> *She's too fat for me.*

There was another one, maybe a little more loving but just as insensitive, called "Hugging and a-Chalking" that celebrated embracing one's way around a bulging girlfriend.

Women, of course, had their place. It was easy enough to see, even in grade school, that girls were generally the best students and stayed that way throughout the higher grades. When they graduated, however, and went to work in a business I noticed they went to the bottom while men went to the top. When I became sensitized to the unfairness of this condition, I tried once to make a change. I gave my boss a schedule that showed how all the women in the department I had taken over were paid less than the men for work that was comparable. He said, yes, that's probably so, but we aren't making a change, that's just the way things are.

Indians were another stereotyped minority. In their case, I believe, society went the other way. From movies, from Boy Scouts, from books, we got the impression they were a silent, noble, courageous people. They had ways of living with nature that we should learn about. We didn't know about cultural alienation, alcoholism, and other problems, and, if we did, they could be forgiven, because, as my father said, "the Indians got a raw deal." When a tall, lean Indian boy transferred into our class in high school, I assumed he would be a good athlete because he looked to me like the great Olympian, Jim Thorpe. It turned out he was about as athletic as most of the rest of us, that is, average.

Then there were the religious proscriptions: Don't attend each other's services. Don't intermarry. Don't read their Bible. Try to convert others; they are not going to heaven. It was as mindless and oppressive as any other prejudice—only this time with the weight of divine retribution.

These were heavy loads that society imposed, but amazingly, in one generation they have been greatly modified. Officially, at least. Not in the behavior of everyone, but in society in general. There has been a revolution in attitudes. It's almost a miracle, you could say. Human beings don't like to change. It took some very brave, early challenges to the prevailing order to make these changes—it took an individual gay person to stand up to ridicule and admit his orientation and demand respect, or a black American to demand service at a segregated lunch counter and another to say there was discrimination in the North as well, or a woman to insist she was qualified and equal. Real acts of courage. Miraculously, it happened without much violence. I experienced these adjustments, sometimes in broad social contexts and sometimes in the small window of my daily activities. I'll never forget going to a civil rights discussion at a Catholic church in Minneapolis in the 1960s, where white people were trying to understand what the black experience was all about. A man in the audience stood up and said, "My name is Bruce Buller, and I can tell you about discrimination. If you want to feel discrimination, try being the pastor of an Evangelical church in St. Cloud, Minnesota." He was serious. I was stunned to hear my hometown mentioned in this context. I didn't learn the details of his experience, but I imagine it came about because a predominantly Catholic civil authority showed no respect for his moral beliefs, which probably concerned drinking, dancing, card playing, and other vices so prevalent in the social order of St. Cloud. We're gathered in this room to consider the great national issue of racial discrimination, I thought, and some man says my hometown has work to do on the subject. No doubt there was truth to what he said. I was learning. On another occasion I was stunned to hear an Indian woman tell me that South Dakota was the most prejudiced state in the nation. More prejudiced than Mississippi? Yes, she said. There must be some real hard feelings behind a statement like that. I was learning.

Now, I think it is safe to say, the prevailing attitudes have changed. Youngsters today seem not to be aware of all the distinctions we made in people. They seem to be willing to let everyone do their own thing. They don't make the categorical judgments we made. Discrimination is illegal, but more than that, it's not cool. I'm sure there are cases of prejudice, but in the broad context we've undergone a marvelous turn of events. I believe the generation I grew up with can take great pride in assisting this movement, this long, difficult journey to tolerance. I believe the word *tolerance* can sum up the great social revolution that took place and that, because of it, we can say with pride that civilization is on a higher plane.

Someday in the future, perhaps this same level of tolerance will prevail throughout the world. If we can imagine such a day, then we can imagine that there will be no need for war. Wouldn't that be a glorious new revolution in values? And the generations who lived through it and helped it come about can stand up in justifiable pride and claim it as theirs. I wish it for my grandchildren.

Epilogue

"AND WHAT IS THE TITLE of your book?" the lady asked from across the table in a noisy restaurant. She did not know me well and was making conversation.

"A Man Learns," I said.

"A Man Yearns?" she asked.

"How do you spell that?" I replied. "U-r-i-n-e-s?"

"No," she said, indignantly. "Y. *Yearns.*"

"Oh." I feigned a new understanding. "No. The title is 'A Man Learns.' *Learns.* But 'Yearns' isn't a bad title either. A man really does yearn. I'll have to think about it."

Indeed, a man yearns. He yearns to understand and to be understood. He yearns for acceptance. He yearns for a full life. He yearns for the goodness of God, although if he's a man on the street he usually doesn't say it in those words. And in all his yearning he is no different from a woman. The book could show that we are the same. Yes, *yearns* would be meaningful; it would be a very nice word for the title.

But because he yearns, a man then learns. He learns the ways of love and understanding and acceptance, and they lead him to the Almighty. If he only yearns, he is incomplete.

A man must *learn* as well. So, *learning* represents accomplishment, although it is never finished. Learning is on a higher level than yearning, and *learns* is what the title will be.

To order additional copies of *A Man Learns*:

Web: www.itascabooks.com

Phone: 1-800-901-3480

Fax: Copy and fill out the form below with credit card information. Fax to 952-920-0541.

Mail: Copy and fill out the form below. Mail with check or credit card information to:

          Syren Book Company
          5120 Cedar Lake Road
          Minneapolis, Minnesota 55416

Order Form

Copies	Title / Author	Price	Totals
	A Man Learns / Donald M. Hall	$14.95	$
	Subtotal		$
	7% sales tax (MN only)		$
	Shipping and handling, first copy		$ 4.50
	Shipping and handling, ___ add'l copies @$1.00 ea.		$
	TOTAL TO REMIT		$

Payment Information:

__ Check Enclosed __ Visa/MasterCard		
Card number: Expiration date:		
Name on card:		
Billing address:		
City:	State:	Zip:
Signature : Date:		

Shipping Information:

__ Same as billing address __ Other (enter below)		
Name:		
Address:		
City:	State:	Zip: